C000137245

Invisible Women

Also by Jacky Trevane

Fatwa

www.fatwajtrevane.com

Invisible Women

True Stories of
Courage and Survival

Jacky Trevane

Hodder & Stoughton
LONDON SYDNEY AUCKLAND

While this book relates true stories, the names of individuals – including the author herself – have been changed to protect those involved and to respect their privacy.

Copyright © 2005 by Jacky Trevane

First published in Great Britain in 2005

The right of Jacky Trevane to be identified as the Author of the Work has been asserted by her in accordance with the Copyright, Designs and Patents Act 1988.

5 7 9 10 8 6 4

British Library Cataloguing in Publication Data
A record for this book is available from the British Library

'For Anne' from *Selected Poems, 1956–1968* by Leonard Cohen.
Used by permission, McClelland & Stewart Ltd.

ISBN 9780340908327

Typeset in Goudy by Avon DataSet Ltd,
Bidford on Avon, Warwickshire

Printed and bound in Great Britain by
Bookmarque Ltd, Croydon, Surrey

The paper and board used in this paperback are natural recyclable products made from wood grown in sustainable forests. The manufacturing processes conform to the environmental regulations of the country of origin.

Hodder & Stoughton
A Division of Hodder Headline Ltd
338 Euston Road
London NW1 3BH
www.madaboutbooks.com

For my mother

'The happiest women, like the happiest nations, have no history.'
George Eliot (Mary Ann Cross), 1819–80

Contents

Prologue   ix
Introduction   xi

1 Reliving the Nightmare   1
2 The Idea   5
3 My Story   10
4 Hounded   18
5 Hunted   29
6 A Friend in Need   36
7 Taking Control   42
8 Moving On   47
9 Empowerment   50
10 Kareena: An Interview   57
11 Laura   72
12 Grace   96
13 Yasmine   121
14 Charlotte   137
15 Shy Girl   161
16 Shannon   215
17 Tamara   243

Acknowledgements   271
Further Help and Information   272

Prologue

We are invisible only for as long as no one can see us.
But that doesn't mean we're not there.
Sometimes right in front of your eyes.
Suffering.
Bleeding inside and out.

But you don't see because you're not looking,
You're too busy to notice.
Preoccupied with the intricacies of your daily routine,
If truth be known
You don't really care enough to scratch away
The fragile exterior covering
The terrible reality
Beneath.

We are everywhere.
Shopping at Sainsbury's,
At the school gate,
Walking in the park,
Cooking dinner.

INVISIBLE WOMEN

We are your mother,
Your niece,
Your best friend,
Your patient,
Your favourite soap star.

Just open your eyes.

Jacky Trevane

Introduction

A lifetime ago, my first husband buried my personality and spirit beneath a thick layer of threats and abuse. Submission, never before apparent in my personality, was soon used as a veil to prevent the outside from looking in and seeing the real me. In effect, I became invisible.

As a wife, submission progressed into resignation. I suffered countless beatings and mental abuse in silence. Only when that violence spread to my daughter did my spirit flare up inside me. I was unable to stand by and tolerate my child suffering too.

As a mother, the instinct to protect my children surmounted any other emotion, and proved to be the catalyst for my rebellion. I struggled to be visible, to escape the life of violence and aggression. To be free.

The escape was successful but, as a result, I had a fatwa, a death threat, placed upon me, which is still with me today. Nevertheless, my two daughters have grown up in a free society, able to express themselves as they wish.

As three liberated women, we can now look back on our struggles with pride. I have written a book about those struggles and set up a website to help other girls in crisis – other girls who, for whatever reason, have also become invisible and wish to tell their stories to an uncaring world.

The enormous response I have received from the website after the publication of *Fatwa: Living with a Death Threat*, inspired me to write my second book, *Invisible Women*, chronicling some of the sad, harrowing and astonishing stories I have been told. They include a Moslem girl reluctant to agree to an arranged marriage; an English girl ostracised and abused by her own family; a girl whose cousin was murdered in an honour killing, wrongly accused of having a boyfriend; and others. From a sometimes unsympathetic, impulsive listener, I have hopefully developed into a more thoughtful, empathic and considerate counterpart, which I've attempted to highlight in the course of the book.

The first story is my own. It tells how I gradually built up a new life and of the events that helped me deal with the fatwa, so that eventually I could let myself embark on a new, fulfilling relationship. That relationship was, and is, everything to me. Through it, I have reaffirmed my faith and strengthened my spirit. It has made me visible again.

1

Reliving the Nightmare

'You should write a book, what with everything that's happened.'

I looked around at the bare, magnolia walls, the little table with the wilting flowers struggling to survive in the hot, cramped space next to a plastic jug half-full of tepid water, a cardboard 'hat' in case of sickness, a wooden spatula and a box of tissues. Mum clutched my hand and my dismissive smile faded as I took in the seriousness of her expression.

'It's all in my head, under control and that's enough for me.' I squeezed her hand gently, not wanting to cause her any distress. Third-time chemotherapy was certainly taking its toll on Mum and I secretly wondered if the accompanying symptoms of distress and sickness were worth it.

'How much do the girls know?' she asked. 'I mean, really know? Does Amira ask about her daddy? You need to think hard, Jacky, and get the whole story down on paper. Look at me. Who would have believed last year that I only had a few more months to live? What if something happens to you?'

1

She leaned back against the crumpled, white pillow, sighing. 'Write it down, darling, write it all down.'

* * *

At home, her words resounded in my head. Through her fatigue she had persisted with the idea, her tired eyes so very earnest. Could I actually write everything down? Could I face it all over again? I put my head in my hands. Mum had never given bad advice. For her sake I had to give it a try.

I began the next day, recording everything chronologically as I remembered the events unfolding. It took ages to start, but after a tentative first couple of paragraphs, I was away, reliving my story. Backache, dry throat and writer's cramp all took second place to my writing. I was inspired. The pages grew with my confidence. I was actually writing a book.

I read each chapter to my mother, sometimes a page at a time when she was too weak to take it all in. She was horrified at some of the details, but overjoyed at the task I had undertaken. She was so proud of me. She tried to concentrate on every sentence, but sadly died three chapters before the end. My spirit died with her.

Six weeks on, I sat down after work one evening, and didn't get up again until those final three chapters had been written, read and rewritten until I was satisfied. I did it for Mum, to keep my word to tell this story from beginning to end. But not just for her. For my two daughters. To know where they came from and why they were born.

And for the thousands of girls who meet the man of their

dreams on holiday and think about marrying that handsome Adonis.

Fatwa: Living with a Death Threat was published early in 2004. I was delighted by the response. The book was reprinted in under six weeks and I even appeared on television, wearing a veil, of course.

In the book I relate the struggles I went through after meeting a dashing Egyptian on holiday, marrying within ten days and living within his culture and religion on the other side of the world. For me this was a huge achievement. Writing a book had been the last thing on my mind two years before when I was visiting my mother. Now two copies had pride of place on the bookcase in the study and there was another in full view in the sitting-room.

Initially, Leila had been shocked and rather unsure at the prospect of her early years being on show to the rest of the world.

'What if my friends read it?' she asked. 'I've never told anyone about that part of our lives. It's so embarrassing, Mum.'

Amira, in contrast, was fascinated. 'Wow, Mum, this is just such a good read. I can hardly believe it's about us. I'd no idea. What a nightmare. It must have taken a lot for you to write it all down. I'm really proud of you.'

Fortunately, Amira's enthusiasm and encouragement prevailed. Within a week she had convinced Leila that the book was not an embarrassment but rather a celebration of how we'd managed to escape across the desert and get home to

England. Leila even began telling her friends proudly that her mum had written a book.

'It's not only a good read, you know,' I heard her say to a friend on her mobile, 'but it'll help loads of other women out there with boyfriends from another country.'

That made me think. If she was right, then could I do even more?

2

The Idea

'Hey, Jacky, quick. Come and see this.'

My husband, lounging on the settee watching the Grand Prix, suddenly sat up and turned up the volume. I nearly fell over in my haste to see what had happened. If it was important enough to get him to sit up, then it must be serious. I took in the bleary, dishevelled features of the man on the screen: Saddam Hussein, found hiding in a hole in the ground. He'd been captured. Such a brutal, cruel tyrant, who had wreaked terror among his own people and brought up his sons to abuse their position of power just as he had done.

What will happen to him now? I wondered.

Whereupon someone grabbed his mouth and probed inside to look at his teeth.

'Unbelievable,' I muttered. 'If things had been the other way around and he had captured one of his enemies, he would have given him a bullet in his head. If he was lucky. What do we do? Check his teeth for fillings.'

'That's our culture, Jacky. You know, the one you risked your life to get back to.'

I looked over at him in amazement. His eyes still on the screen, he located his pint of Guinness expertly and finished it off. He had no idea how profoundly that simple statement had affected me.

The newsflash ended and I wandered back into the kitchen to check on the Yorkshire puddings. It smelt lovely in there, meaty and warm, a typical Sunday dinner. I stirred the gravy, thinking about what Ben had said. He was right, of course. Saddam had complete cultural autonomy; he abused his power, and his people, out of fear, accepted it. Like me. Trapped in an abusive marriage in a foreign country, I had been subjected to frequent abuse and, out of fear, I accepted it. Submissively. Saddam once had a whole nation in the palm of his hand, and it was worse, far worse for the women. They lived in constant fear of abuse and experienced little or no respect. Maybe things would start to change for them with him gone. I really hoped so.

Later, sitting at the table during lunch, I looked around at all the faces, chatting, asking for more. A warm, comfortable feeling rushed through me. Fifteen years earlier, reduced to a wretched state with a bleak future ahead of us, I'd risked everything to escape from Egypt with my two daughters and we had been lucky to have made it. But at the time, all those years ago, I had told no one. I had put on the polite mask each day, as if everything was fine. I was invisible then. Like thousands of other women. Hidden by the veil. Abused in communities across the world and across Britain. What did

it matter? No one raised their voice in protest. No one knew.
No one saw.

'But I'm not now.'

'What, Mum?'

The conversations dwindled as I realised they were all
looking at me expectantly. I must have said it out loud.

'Oh, nothing. Pass the mustard, please.'

That's when I had the idea.

*　　*　　*

Later that day I wandered over to the bookcase, took down
a copy of *Fatwa*, and leafed steadily through the pages.

'Ben, how easy is it to set up a website?'

'Oh, no, she's got another idea.' He rolled his eyes
dramatically and sat up, pushing the cat off his knee. 'What
is it this time? Speed dating? Safari holidays?' Laughing he
put his arms tightly round me. 'So go on, spill the beans.'

'I was thinking.'

'And . . . ?'

'About me. The desperate state I was in, how persecuted
I used to be, how hopeless everything seemed.'

'Jacky, no. You've come through that. You're here with
me now. The girls are safe and well.' He smoothed my
hair out of my face and kissed me. 'I knew writing the
book would bring it all back. But you have to try and focus
on the life we've built up since then and look forward.
Okay?'

'But that's the whole point. Yes, I have come through it.
I was as low as a human being could ever be. Yet I got

through it. Life was a punishment, a sentence I had to serve. And today I'm standing here with you.'

He grinned. He knew exactly what I meant.

'I walk around with a smile on my face. I appreciate everything we have. Every day is precious and I will never, ever take things for granted.' I pushed away from his grasp and swirled around in front of him. 'Just look at me now. I love life. I'm happy, in love and completely fulfilled. Who would have believed it?'

I took his hand, pulled him into the bedroom and pushed him onto the bed. 'Wait there. I want to show you something.'

Pulling a folder from the bottom drawer of my desk, I took it through to him and spread the contents onto the bed.

'Look. Letters. From girls and women all over the world who have read my book.'

Ben picked them up, skimming through the contents. He was amazed. 'These are brilliant, Jacky. Not one of them criticises you, they're all genuinely complimentary. And look at some of their own stories.' He lay back, absorbed in his reading.

'You see? They're everywhere. Women suffering. Women accepting their lot without question. Women who have lost their identity and become invisible. So I got to thinking that maybe I could help.'

'And this is your great idea?' Ben looked unconvinced, but I could see he was weakening.

'Yes.' I bounced on the bed, ignoring his tone. 'If I had a website, girls could contact me to get in touch with other girls with similar problems or just to pour their hearts out. It's such a good idea, Ben, don't you think?' I grabbed his arm excitedly.

'What use is advice from a stranger? What makes you think you could do anything to make any one of their lives easier? No, Jacky. Sorry, but I think you've got your head in the clouds.'

'Typical male response. Well, you're not going to put me off. This is a great way for me to do my bit for other women out there. All they need is a glimmer of hope. Simply knowing that someone cares enough to listen is enough. It would have been for me. If I can actually reach out to some of these poor girls then I will.'

'Why am I not surprised?' said Ben as he methodically replaced the letters into the folder. 'Come on then. Let's build a bloody website then. I can see there's no use in arguing.'

3

My Story

It's not a condition, invisibility. Not something you are one minute that changes the next. It's more like a symptom or a process. A symptom of continual oppression and abuse, when instead of standing up for yourself, you begin to submit, to give in and start backing away. When you back right into the corner, when there is no further retreat, you begin to shrink until gradually your spirit breaks and you are no longer you. You become invisible.

The irony is in the fact that it's so easy. Rebellion is harder, always stressful, sometimes terrifying. The fear factor is powerful; if you submit then maybe he won't hit you quite so hard / trash the house / go crazy. Much better to shut up, take it on the chin, back off and submit. Don't rock the boat.

Gradually it's bye-bye confidence, opinions, personality, smiles. Nerves on edge, bitten fingernails, skulking around? Look in the mirror. Who do you see? A faceless stranger? Hi. It's the new you. You're one of us now. Invisible women.

For me, it was a slow process. About five years, all told. My second daughter was still a baby. By then I had been punched and kicked black and blue, suffered an enforced miscarriage, been raped by my husband's brother and beaten again for complaining about it. My ribs had been broken and my British passport – my identity – had been wrenched from my hands in a terrible fight that resulted in yet another stay in the horrible government hospital for the poor, to tend my broken ribs. I had evolved into a powerless state of nothingness. An invisible woman. I was numb, deadened, dehumanised.

We are all familiar with the saying, 'Everything happens for a reason.' And it is only now, sixteen years later, that I can begin to appreciate this.

I made the conscious decision to marry a handsome, romantic Egyptian in the full knowledge that this would mean living as an English wife of a Moslem within an alien culture. Having absolutely no prior knowledge of their traditions, language or religion, I rushed into the marriage, seduced by his beautiful brown eyes and constant reassurances that all we would ever ultimately need was each other.

Foolhardy. Thoughtless. Selfish. Unbelievably immature. Naïve. Gullible. All wonderfully appropriate adjectives to describe this decision and every one of them true. I was intelligent, articulate and fully able to rationalise and appraise my decisions from an objective standpoint. Yet when it came to the most important decision of my life up until that time, all notions of rationality flew straight out of the window. I threw myself into an unknown, uncertain future.

My hopes and ambitions were short-lived. He was unsympathetic to my struggles, and scathing of my efforts to be a good wife. When things went smoothly he said nothing, yet if I forgot something or made even the smallest mistake, his dark eyes filled with anger and he flew into a rage, hitting or biting me. In a sick sort of way, he almost seemed to enjoy the feeling of his teeth sinking into my soft, white flesh and hearing my desperate screams. He never once gave me the chance to explain. His behaviour developed into a pattern: hit first, calm down and apologise later. I began to judge his mood by his eyes. They were no longer sultry, deep and seductive; only terrifying and wild.

What was I expecting? A challenge certainly. I listened eagerly to the Arabic language and learned as much as I could about Islam. The experience could have been magical and enriching. I was ready and willing to learn everything about this foreign land and adopt the habits and attitudes expected of a Moslem wife. I actually read the Qu'ran from beginning to end and eventually came to understand and respect this wonderfully complicated religion. I knew that men in power used Islam as a weapon and ultimately as justification for their actions. They interpreted or rather misinterpreted the teachings so that they supported whatever they wanted to do.

There are countless examples of this all over the world. Saddam Hussein, Osama Bin Laden, the Taliban, the honour assassins, the barbarians who still butcher little girls, circumcising them 'in the name of Islam'. It's happening now.

Today, in the twenty-first century. It's even happening here, in England.

Yet, as my story unfolds, there comes with it the terrifying irony and realisation that I understand and respect Islam more than the people who brought it to my attention. My husband used the religion for his own ends, hitting me and excusing his anger and violence by blaming me for disrespecting the laws of Islam. He followed the teachings as long as it suited him and he appeared pious to outsiders. I see this very clearly now. His sister was a wonderful example of a true Moslem, putting her faith and the beliefs first, and living her life within those limits.

In contrast, my husband – that is, my ex-husband – manipulated his religion to make it acceptable to dominate, disrespect and ultimately abuse me. I was unable to fight back. A Christian, European female married to a Moslem, living within the confines of a poor Moslem family in their country. Rights? What rights? I was no less than scum in that department.

As a result, my confidence deserted me, along with hope, faith and eventually love for my handsome, brown-eyed husband. I lost my sense of self, accepting blame and recriminations, even chastising myself after a beating, determined to try harder so that he wouldn't get angry next time. Then things would be all right. I began to shrink, not even daring to think that I was ever right.

At first, everything had seemed like a wonderful dream. I'd gone on a chartered flight to Cairo with my boyfriend,

Dave, and on the first day, travelling on a crowded bus, we managed to lose each other. I hurt my ankle, having fallen out of the bus, while Dave had mistakenly got off at the stop before. That bus journey was the last time we saw each other until we met up again at the airport to go home ten days later. But it was far too late to patch up this already rocky relationship. I held out my left hand to reveal the shiny, new gold band on the third finger: I had married someone else.

Omar was attentive, adoring and extremely good-looking, possessing that presence and self-confidence most good-looking men have. He lived with his parents in a ground-floor flat on the outskirts of the city. They were non-English-speaking, except for his younger sister, Salma, who did a brilliant job of translating and making me feel as comfortable as possible. Yet the honeymoon was soon over as I struggled to cope with a life which was different in every way to the one I had left behind.

Try as I might, I made mistakes until Omar revealed his dark side and began to punish me with vicious punches or savage bites. It was pointless to resist. He was stronger and I lived in fear of his black moods and sudden brutal out-bursts. We had a daughter, Leila, and I managed to get a teaching job in an English school to bring in some money.

That was the other thing. Money. We didn't have any. I had believed his stories of a Mercedes and a building company plus several apartment blocks. He had given me the impression that life in their beautiful, romantic country would be a lifelong holiday.

Reality hit hard. No Mercedes. No car at all, in fact. His father owned a white Peugeot estate which Omar sometimes borrowed. In fact Omar had been lying about everything. He himself owned nothing and earned nothing. He was a student, relying totally on his family for his every need. His father did own a business of sorts. 'The building company' was a shed in a remote village where they made cupboards and the odd chair for the lower classes. The apartment block was an unfinished six-storey building housing twelve flats in a poor area called Embaba, where children ran around barefoot in the dust with flies crawling all over their faces and eyes, and their mothers, swathed in black, drew water from the handpump in the street. On the ground floor of the building was another workshop, a dusty, filthy space which he called his 'company'. This was filled with wood stacked along the walls and a few primitive tools. There was no electricity.

I fell pregnant within the first few months and was delighted to be allowed to travel back to England for the birth after my father sent the air fare. At home, I revelled in the comforts of hot baths, walking in the park, baked beans, hoovering, ironing, eating at the table with a knife and fork. In Egypt, no one had baths, only showers. In the flat where I had moved, we didn't even have water in the taps, let alone hot water. There were no parks, unless you were rich enough to pay to belong to a club like the Gezira, where it was acceptable for women to meet for lunch and let their children run on the grass and play on the swings. Without the money to join such a ritzy establishment, opportunities for the lower classes to enjoy such amenities were limited, although the zoo was very popular, filled with Friday trippers picnicking and making the most of it. The only beans we could afford were called *fool*, which we bought from the street vendor every morning: dark brown, bland and tasteless. We had to add salt to make them edible. Of course, baked beans did exist in Cairo, but only in the supermarkets and were way out of our financial reach. In all the eight and a half years I was in Egypt, I could never afford to shop in a supermarket. So we managed with *fool*.

As for hoovering or ironing, these pleasures did not exist in my husband's family household. First, only rich people afforded carpets, *moquette*, as they called it. We had thin rugs which were shaken and hung over the balcony daily until after siesta, when they were replaced in time to eat.

All meals were eaten sitting on the floor with spoons and all the crumbs and mess would be flung into the street without a care for the unsuspecting passers-by. This negated the need for a hoover. The ironing was sent to a *macwaggi*, an ironing man. He used an ancient iron, heated on hot coals. The shirts were always immaculate yet he was paid a pittance for his trouble.

From the beginning, my marriage was challenging and often daunting. I had experienced the rage of my father-in-law and had certainly seen a different side to Omar. But I wasn't ready to quit. Not yet. I still loved him passionately. Refusing to see the situation in its stark reality, I made excuses for both him and his family's aggression towards me, laying the blame at my own door each time.

Returning after the birth of Leila, I managed to unleash Omar's terrible anger again and again, until being hit became part of my routine, almost accepted. I lived in fear, telling no one, pretending we were the perfect couple. I had another daughter, Amira.

It was only when some English friends of my parents, Val and Dave Hargreaves, visited that I saw a glimmer of hope. I had been locked in the flat after a beating around my face. That day, I was so low, I just wanted to die. When Val knocked on the door and saw my injuries through the little window, I decided to ask her for help.

It was the turning-point. To avoid suspicion, I met them at the school where I worked. We hatched a complicated escape plan and I spent the next four months preparing for that day.

Keep Hubby up late, rise early, dress kids for a normal school day. Tell bus driver not to expect you due to wedding, go to bus station in friend's car. Give Leila change of clothes and school clothes to friend for her daughter on way. Buy return tickets to Israel to avoid suspicion. Bus to Israel, through Egyptian border. Hotel near airport. Tickets bought by Dave Hargreaves waiting for me. Reverse charges call to parents to say things were going to plan. Plane from Israel to London. Home.

4

Hounded

Actually, it all sounds so simple. It wasn't. In the heat of the blazing sun, we crossed the desert from Egypt to Israel and suffered unending questions and bullying from Mossad, the Israeli secret police. I had so little money that we had to last two days on a bottle of water and a box of cheese triangles. I quaked with fear every step of the way. It was traumatic and utterly nerve-racking, but in the end we were running into the arms of my parents. They were meeting two-year-old Amira for the first time.

'Thank the Lord,' my mother gasped through her sobs, burying her tear-stained face deep into Amira's thick, curly mop of auburn hair. Leila ran up to hug her grandad, leaving me standing alone, looking on, wondering when I was going to wake up. We couldn't have made it. This was a beautiful dream. This couldn't be real. Good things just didn't happen to us. Happy endings were for books, in fairy tales. Vaguely I registered Amira dragging Mum across the vast hall towards a shop. I felt a tugging on my sleeve.

'Hug Grandad, Mama.'

Instinctively, my finger was up to my lips in an automatic

gesture to warn her of the danger of speaking English. It lasted only a fraction of a second as my dad wrapped his huge arms around me in a bear hug. He wept into my neck, his tears trickling onto my blouse. I clutched him tightly, crying silently, shaking inside, inhaling his smell. And I knew.

We *had* made it. My dad smelt of soap and Persil, the washing powder Mum always used, bringing back memories of home and childhood, comfort and kindness.

'Mama, Mama, *hodi*, Mama.'

Quickly wiping away my tears, I turned to see little Amira running towards me, with Mum in tow, a bunch of flowers in her hand, so big that she was almost hidden from view.

'*Hodi*, Mama. *Shoofi wearda.*'

'It's okay, Jacky, I've paid for them. She was adamant about having them. What is she saying?'

Smiling, I bent to retrieve the flowers, heavy in her tiny hands, explaining to Mum, 'She said, "Take these, Mama. Look at the flowers." ' Still crouching at her level, I thanked Amira. '*Shokran, habibti. Hellwa awy. Hellwa giddan.*'

'Does she understand any English, then?' Dad asked Leila.

'Amira speak little. She's still baby. Papa wants Arabic only.' Leila's own reply was stilted.

The only opportunity to speak English was at school or if we were left alone in the house, and even then I had to be careful not to overdo it. If Leila slipped up and lapsed into English by accident when Papa was at home, he would fly into a rage and beat me for disobeying him. Leila was fiercely

19

protective of me at all times and very, very careful to behave in a quiet, respectful way in the presence of her father. She had learned not to do things that could antagonise or provoke his temper. Already she was growing into an invisible woman. At six.

Now, she went up to Amira and calmly told her that they should now only speak English, to respect Nanna and Grandad, who could not understand Arabic.

As I translated for my parents, more tears rolled down my cheeks. How mature and unconditionally accepting of the situation it was for such a little girl.

'I'll teach you everything. Don't worry,' she said, still in Arabic. Pointing to the flowers, she said, 'Flowers. Flo-wers. Say it. Flo-wers.'

'Fowers.'

At which, Leila laughed delightedly and swung her sister round until they both collapsed on the floor, giggling.

I looked from them to my parents. 'I think we're going to be fine.'

* * *

That was the last time Leila spoke Arabic in her life. Amira didn't need explanations. She copied us and quickly took in the language around her. Without hearing Arabic, she was able to discard it. In Egypt, this had also happened to Leila, only the other way round. She had become fluent in Arabic and lost fluency in English when it was decided by the family that this was no longer a desirable skill. She would speak only in their language, or suffer the consequences.

So it was doubly hard for Leila to stop communicating in the only language she really felt confident with. If I spoke to her in Arabic to help her understand, she would completely ignore me and pretend I had not spoken. This was a complex, mature decision she had made independently and one that she has always kept to.

On the journey to my parents' house in the car, I explained to both the children that Nanna and Grandad's home would also be ours until I could find a place for the three of us. As it was important they both fully understood that this was not just a holiday, I spoke in Arabic. I had just started when Leila angrily interrupted.

'No, Mama. English now. Stop. Talk English.' She stared at me, her eyes unwavering, full of meaning.

'Of course, darling. In English.'

So I did just that. I explained that we could never return to Egypt, not even for a holiday, and we would never see Papa again. I smoothed Leila's hair from her face. This was a brutal statement and would probably upset her, but I knew I had to make it clear from the beginning before we could move on as a different family unit, this time with me at the head.

She threw her arms around me, kissed me and pushed up my sleeve to reveal a large purple bruise. She bent and kissed this also, stroking it and looking quietly up at me. 'No more, Mama?'

'No more, *habibti*.'

As her face darkened, I realised my mistake. 'No more, darling.'

'English, Mama.'

'Ingish,' repeated Amira solemnly, not to be left out.

* * *

The next week was fraught with tension. It took Omar a couple of days to realise that somehow, even though he had my passport locked up or burnt most likely, we had managed to leave the country. It wouldn't have occurred to him at first, especially as Amira was his insurance against this. Leila had been born in England and I had her British birth certificate. Amira, born in Egypt, had an Egyptian birth certificate, which I had never even seen, and I certainly had no knowledge of its whereabouts. There was no way I could travel unless I left her behind. Or so he assumed.

Having bombarded all my friends and colleagues several times to no avail, he became almost delirious with anger and frustration. Most of my teaching friends had no idea of my plans and were being honest when he questioned them. The two girls who did know remained tight-lipped, although Jill later wrote to me, saying how Omar had lost his cool and revealed his darker side when they didn't tell him what he wanted to know.

'It was awful, Jacky,' she wrote. 'At first he was the charming, polite Omar we have always known. But when he returned on the second day, he showered us with accusations and threats. My husband took him into the front room and asked me to make some tea. He was obviously trying to calm Omar down, but I could hear them arguing and shouting. When I went into the room with the tea, I was really shocked. Omar had lost control. It was frightening. You should have seen his eyes. Black with fury. Methad took the tea from me and indicated that I should leave. I didn't need telling twice. Omar ignored the tea and stormed out. He punched the door on his way out and managed to splinter the wood. Can you believe it?'

'Oh yes, that's my Omar,' I whispered to myself.

Two days later, after finding no answers to his questions, Omar had nowhere else to look and it dawned on him that I had not run away to a friend's house on a whim. This would have been the perfect excuse for him to punish me with beating after beating and even more restrictions. He would have loved the chance to reaffirm his power by 'disciplining' me after such a misdemeanour.

The phone calls began on the third day after our escape.

The telephone system then in Cairo was very unreliable. I had rarely made calls to England from Cairo, and it was necessary to go through the operator. Even then the lines were usually crackling with background noise or other people on crossed lines trying to get through to someone else. It was rare if you could speak for more than a few minutes without being cut off. The result was that Omar started phoning day and night, trying to establish where we were. We appointed Dad to handle the phone. After several crackly calls in the middle of the night, when it was easy to disconnect without saying anything, we realised that Omar was not going to give up.

'I suppose it's time to tell him where you are.' Dad, sitting up in bed, looked from Mum to me.

'Are you sure? What will he do if he knows we're here? He knows this address and phone number.' I began to shake. Even across a fuzzy phone line four thousand miles away, Omar still made me shiver with fear.

My Dad smiled. 'What *can* he do? He'll most likely want to do plenty, fly over here and take you back. But he can't actually do it. First, you wouldn't agree. Second, you're a British citizen and he cannot force you to go. No, the best thing is to speak to him.'

'What . . . ?'

'Not you,' he added hurriedly, seeing my horrified expression.

Mum leaned forward anxiously. 'Don't give away too much, for goodness' sake. Decide what you're going to say, write it down and stick to it.'

And that's what we did. While Leila and Amira slept peacefully through the night, we huddled together in the hall by the phone with mugs of hot chocolate, waiting for the next call. Sure enough, it came through half an hour later. Omar's voice, asking for me, very politely.

'Good evening. This is Jacky's father. Jacky is safe and well. She and the girls will be living in England from now on. Please do not contact us again. Jacky does not wish to speak to you. Goodbye.'

Dad replaced the receiver firmly and turned to us. 'There is nothing more we need say to him,' he said. 'Nothing at all.'

*   *   *

Of course that didn't placate Omar in the slightest. He continued to call, at all hours, but we refused to receive the calls. It was all taking its toll on us. We felt hounded, never free of the endless ringing of the phone. We decided that it would be foolish to change the number at this stage, as it was more important to know what mood Omar was in and what his plans were. But the worry and stress were certainly getting to us.

Then the letters started. Long, rambling letters in broken English. Letters begging for our return, full of apologies and promises of a wonderful future with him, no more violence, no more vile moods. How much he loved and missed us. How he couldn't bear the thought of another day without us. How there could never be anyone else for him. On and on he rambled, each letter three or four sides of paper, his small handwriting covering every inch.

After the first dozen or so, I stopped reading them. Omar wasn't stupid. He knew how to get to me. With such a distance between us, his tactic was now to constantly bombard me with letters and calls, to never give up until he'd got his own way and I relented. He knew by doing this he would prevent me from moving on and that eventually I would break and submit. We would go back to him. *Then* I would pay.

Not this time. Mum monitored the letters. Dad refused the calls.

In less than three weeks, the tone of the letters changed.

With no response from us, Omar now launched into torrents of abuse, laced with threats. No longer tolerant of my 'disobedience', he threatened to force me to return. He would send someone to kidnap the girls and wait for me to follow of my own accord to be with them. He had 'contacts' in England who could help him with anything he wanted.

Arab families were often extensive and remained loyal and interconnected. A poor boy from a remote village might well have a wealthy uncle, four times removed, who was living in Europe and would be willing to help him. Not necessarily financially, but to give him a bed to sleep in and advice or contacts to enable him to find work. As the victim of gross betrayal by an infidel who had 'stolen' his children, there would be a lot of people prepared to help such a 'good Moslem' as Omar.

'Oh my God, he's going to take the girls.' I was out of my mind with worry. I was fully aware of the extent of Omar's anger. All reason flew out of the window when he was pursuing something.

'We'll be waiting for him,' Dad said, a grim smile on his face. 'You'd better visit a solicitor, Jacky.'

The next day, I did just that and made both girls Wards of Court. I took Omar's letters and tried to start divorce proceedings, but came up against a problem. I just couldn't recall the bad times. Not specifically anyway. The details were blurred. I struggled to say anything and eventually broke down and cried. To cite unreasonable behaviour, it was necessary to give some sort of evidence.

At home, I stood at the cooker making dinner, discussing it with my mother.

'How can I make myself remember, Mum? It must be some sort of self-defence mechanism. In Egypt, I used to pretend the bad times were a dream, or happening to someone else. I don't think I'll ever be able to remember even one occasion when he hit me.'

'I can remember everything, Mama.' Leila, standing quietly in the doorway, had heard it all.

I looked round at her. It had been my little six-year-old who had given me the strength and courage to flee from Egypt. I remembered the first time I had looked on in horror as my husband viciously slapped her legs for some minor, insignificant infraction and heard her cry out in surprise. My clearest memory was of the day when she was standing up in her cot, around eighteen months old, and Papa lifted her up by her ear. She screamed, but then, through her tears, saw me approaching to help her. In that moment she put her little arms up, shaking her finger, saying, '*La'a*, mama, *la'a*' ('No, mummy, no'). She knew what happened if I ever tried to intervene: I was punched hard in my stomach and face. She was more concerned about Papa hurting Mama, than Papa hurting Leila. Even then she was protecting me. I knew I had to get her out of his reach. Now in England, Leila continued to assume the role of protector.

She sat in the solicitor's office the next day, hands folded on the desk and asked the solicitor how much he wanted to know. She managed the whole conversation in almost perfect

English. It was frightening to realise that nothing that had gone on between Mama and Papa in that dusty, half-built flat in Egypt had escaped her eyes and ears. It made me see that by the age of six, children are far more knowledgeable and therefore more deeply affected by family violence and strife than we would ever suspect. Not all Egyptian men are the same. But my brutal husband had created a family setting that was vile and deeply disturbing. I could do nothing, living within a culture that condoned such behaviour as the natural rights of a husband and head of his family.

After an hour of consultation, the case was complete. Leila was calm and composed. I was an emotional wreck. Her tales had forced me to confront my past and open the black boxes filed away in a dark corner of my mind.

'Come on, Mama. It's okay now.' She grasped my hand and stood up, ready to leave.

'Thank you.' I shook hands with the solicitor.

'You have a very astute daughter. I'll be in touch. Goodbye.'

5

Hunted

In the weeks that followed, we tried to establish routines for the girls to help them settle more easily into their new surroundings. Leila was enrolled at the local primary school. The other children were fascinated by her stilted English. Rather than ostracise her, they wanted to be her friend and include her in their games. A month later, all traces that Leila might not be English had vanished. Already she was developing into a happy, more relaxed child, shedding the anxieties of the past and the awful responsibility of protecting me.

When Mum's sister, Auntie Joyce, visited and asked Leila about school, she talked animatedly about her school day.

'Oh, it's very different from Egypt. Here we can talk.'

'What do you mean? Surely you were allowed to talk?' Auntie Joyce was fascinated.

Leila shook her head. 'But here we talk and no one shouts at us. We can ask questions if we get stuck and the teacher tells us what to do. I like the big room best.'

'The big room?'

'Yes,' replied Leila. 'Every day we walk in a long line to

the big room. We have to sit on the floor and Mrs Sanderson comes to talk to us. Then she says we have to put our hands together and close our eyes. When she says, "Ahem", we can open them again.'

Auntie Joyce laughed. 'It's called assembly, darling.'

Leila nodded. 'Yes, that's it. I forgot.'

'You close your eyes for the prayer. And it's "Amen", not "Ahem". That's what you say at the end.' She smiled. 'Do you ever peep?'

Leila looked horrified. 'Of course not,' she replied indignantly.

Amira was feisty, independent and strong. She loved Leila with a passion, copying her in everything she did and following her around adoringly. This annoyed Leila, who considered herself far too grown-up to be going around with a two-year-old. Anyway, she now had a whole classful of new friends. This resulted in Leila being insensitive and often cruel towards her little sister, pushing her away, shouting at her, even hitting her. She had grown up with violence and would have to learn that this was not the norm.

Sibling rivalry. A new experience for me. I was an only child. In Egypt, they had only each other; their friends at school had never been allowed to come round to play. School friends were for school and home was for each other. Now the two were crossing over and Amira was being pushed out.

We found the answer in the Mother and Toddler Group, twice a week. I met a few other mums and invited a couple of friends home to play with Amira. She was then invited back. When Amira stopped following Leila around from dawn till dusk, Leila decided Amira wasn't such a nuisance after all, and the problem I'd seen as huge gradually disappeared.

Meanwhile, I had changed our surname through a solicitor. This would make it more difficult for Omar to find us. I had to make a Statutory Declaration; with Deed Poll, both parents needed to be informed. I let Leila choose it at random from the phone book. Bailey. Leila understood and was proud of our new name.

This proved to be completely fruitless. When the divorce papers were finally delivered into Omar's hands via an English firm of solicitors in Cairo, I was named as Jacky Bailey. The Decree Nisi and a bungling clerk had blown my cover.

Omar took great pleasure in sending a hate-filled letter, gloating that I would never be able to hide. He had ripped up the divorce papers and said he would never divorce me. Ever.

Simply by accepting them on his doorstep, however, meant that the papers had been served. The fact that he disagreed was irrelevant. Although he now knew I was trying to hide from him by changing my name, there was nothing he could do about our divorce. The Decree Nisi went through, as did the Decree Absolute six weeks later. By then, I had changed our surname again, through a solicitor, to Thompson.

Omar remained furious and full of revenge. The phone

calls had become sporadic and therefore more tolerable. I never bent to his pleading. I would never speak to him, no matter how much he begged, wept or threatened. Never.

His letters, however, continued to drop through the letterbox at the rate of three a week, often arriving together. They were evidence of his wild mood swings. One minute he was offering me the world, saying he had bought two ponies for the girls. The next, vowing to snatch the girls and keep them away from me forever. Mum never read the letters out, merely gave me the gist. That way, I knew what state of mind he was in and how it might affect us.

After news of the divorce, his reply was that under Egyptian law we were still married. I had humiliated him and I would pay.

'Mum, I'm worried. He means business this time. I can feel it.'

'No, love. He's just trying to frighten you.'

I took the letter from her. 'Only three lines. Usually he crams words into every space on the page. He's going to do something.'

* * *

Four days later, the phone rang. Dad answered, and a man with a foreign accent uttered the chilling words, 'I am calling from London with a message for Jacky from Omar. He has obtained passports for his daughters and is coming to take them back to Egypt. You have no choice in this matter.'

Dad replaced the receiver and sat down heavily. 'This is

getting serious, Jacky. We must be able to protect you somehow. Can he do this?'

'I don't think so,' I replied. We'll just have to be extra careful.'

We informed the local police and contacted the Home Office. If Omar succeeded in obtaining a visa, then he was legally entitled to come to England. But he had no right to take the girls anywhere now they were Wards of Court.

Would that stop him? I wondered. He wouldn't come all this way and leave without them. He'd make some plan to snatch them. I was sure of it.

I took Leila to school the following morning and explained that only my mother or me should pick her up and that she should not leave with anyone else. Also, if anyone made any inquiries at all about her, I should be telephoned immediately. I started the speech on strangers with Leila, but she interrupted.

'I understand, Mama. No one will ever take me away. No one.'

Then another letter informed me that Omar had visited an imam, a religious leader, who had imposed a fatwa on me. This was a decree giving Omar permission to kill me or have me killed for my sins against him. In Egypt, I had converted to Islam in order to remain with my children in case anything happened to Omar and also in my untiring efforts to be the proper, obedient wife he so desired. A fatwa can be issued only against a Moslem, and Omar had used this against me. My sins? Leaving my husband without his permission, travelling unescorted out of the country and taking his daughters away from him. Sufficient for the death sentence. We had to take this as a serious threat, not to be ignored.

'Bloody hell. How far is that bastard prepared to go? If I could get my hands on him . . .'

'Don't, darling. Don't let him get to you.' Mum squeezed my father's arm meaningfully.

'Don't let him get to me? You are joking, aren't you? You're telling me that some jumped-up ponce over there has the right to say that bastard can murder my daughter? My God, not if I get to him first.'

Dad was shaking with rage. He was an emotional man and often got upset over trivial things, but it was very unusual to hear him swear. He disapproved of profanities, in films or songs. He was very articulate and certainly didn't beat about the bush. 'Swearing's for inadequate morons who can neither express nor control themselves. There's absolutely no justification for it.'

Mum and Dad put their home up for sale that day. No tears, recriminations or regrets. The decision was made quickly and easily. They had to protect their daughter, and moving away would certainly help. I was speechless. It had been our family home for thirty years. The guilt and pain I felt was indescribable. But I knew Omar's threats were real. *He would not hesitate to kill me if he could get to me.* A chill ran through me.

A letter from the Home Office confirmed my worst fears.

Omar had forged a letter to him from me, inviting him to visit us in England. With the letter, he was intending to obtain a visa to travel. The Home Office had the foresight to check that the letter was authentic, and asked me how long he was expecting to stay. I was so grateful for their thoroughness. I telephoned immediately to deny all knowledge of the letter and put the Home Office fully in the picture. Omar's plan had been foiled. We were safe. For today.

But now I found myself looking behind me constantly. Gradually I changed from an outgoing, sociable girl into a quieter, less spontaneous person, forever watchful, like the invisible woman I'd been in the filthy backstreets of Cairo. Not that there was any point in looking over my shoulder, as I had no idea what I was looking for. But I still did it, over and again.

6

A Friend in Need

I had no money and no income. Mum and Dad had unquestioningly fed, clothed and supported all three of us. It was time for me to give something back. The options were limited. The dole? A council house? Teaching? I had taught in Egypt, but with only a qualification in Teaching English as a Foreign Language. To be able to teach in England I would have to take a Postgraduate Certificate in Education.

'It's okay, Jacky. Go for it. I'll take care of the kids. You can come back and relieve me at weekends.'

I stared at Mum. She really meant it. She was prepared to give up her home, her life as she knew it, *and* take on the kids for a year until I qualified to teach.

Dad nodded at her words. 'We're not as young as we were. But we'll do our best. Just get yourself qualified.'

It was May. There were sixty-five colleges around the country offering the course. The closing date for applications had been the previous October. Undeterred, Dad went out and bought some new stationery. He paid for sixty-five stamps and we sent the applications off. Only two of the replies were positive, each offering me an interview. I attended the first in the north of England, was offered a place and accepted it straightaway.

It was an eventful year. Working in a bar on weekday nights, living above a shop with another mature student who also went home at weekends to her children, there was no time to socialise with other students. The work was challenging and time-consuming, with numerous deadlines to meet. Every weekend I went home and spent time with Leila and Amira. Leila turned seven and later, Amira three. Mum and Dad moved to a new home, leaving their old address and telephone number behind them. Without telling me, Dad arranged with Philomena and Richard, the new owners, for all letters from Egypt to be put to one side for him to collect. They told me later that this was to keep check on what was going on.

Believing that Omar had finally given up on us, I started to relax. I qualified, returned to the new house, managed to get a local teaching job and secured a mortgage on a terraced house in town. The girls and I settled into our new life together.

Then one day, I bumped into an old school-friend. It was great to see her. She was reeling after finding out her husband was having an affair with her best friend.

'He's been gone for a couple of months now,' she said. 'Come out with me, Jacky. I need a night out.'

I hadn't been 'out' for years. Pubs and clubs meant only one thing to me: men. A commodity I had long decided I could do without. But Hazel brushed away my concerns and persuaded me to do a friend a good turn.

Pubs had certainly changed since I was a teenager. Flower power, long skirts and patchouli had been replaced by belts passing themselves off as skirts, tiny backless dresses and hair braids. In my jeans and blouse, I felt overdressed, old-fashioned and, at thirty-one, positively the oldest female on the planet.

'Some of these girls can't be more than thirteen or fourteen,' I shouted to Hazel above the music. 'Where do their parents think they are?'

She shrugged. 'God, this place is packed. How do we get a drink in here?'

I looked around. 'Stay here. Won't be long.'

Making sure I had about the right amount of change for our drinks, I watched one of the barmaids serve a guy three rows in front. Pushing towards him, I managed to reach out and prod him on the shoulder. 'Excuse me. Can I be cheeky and ask if you'd add two halves of lager and a packet of crisps to your order? I've got the right money here.'

He turned and smiled. 'Sure. No problem. Where are you standing?'

'Over by the window. Thanks.'

Ten minutes later we were standing with our order in front of us. With a smile, the guy disappeared into the crowd.

'Wow, Jacky. Clever plan. Bold as brass, aren't you?' Hazel winked at me, sipping her drink.

'Actually, I'm quite proud of myself,' I replied. 'Oh no,

the guy, you know, the one who brought the drinks? He's coming over.'

'Hi, how's it going?' he asked, looking directly at Hazel.

'All right now, thanks to you,' she replied, smiling.

'They fancy each other,' I thought. 'Result: time to make yourself scarce, Jacky Thompson.'

I escaped to the loo, taking much longer than was necessary and returned to see them on the dance floor, obviously enjoying themselves. After a couple of tracks they joined me.

'Thanks, Hazel. I'll see you around.' He turned to me. 'Nice to meet you, Jacky.' And he was gone.

'He seemed nice,' I said.

'Glad *you* think so,' said Hazel.

'Why? Didn't you get on?'

'Didn't get the chance.'

'What? I watched you dancing and you were chatting nineteen to the dozen.'

'If you must know, he was asking me about you,' she replied.

'Me?'

'It's not rocket science, Jacky. It's not me he's interested in, it's you. How do you think he knew your name?'

'Well, I hope you told him I'm not interested and never will be.'

'You can tell him yourself. He was so persistent that in the end I gave him your folks' telephone number.'

I choked on my drink. 'You did what?'

'Oh, come on, he was nice. What harm can there be in talking to him?'

Suddenly the room was stifling. I couldn't breathe. 'Let's go home.'

'What's wrong with you, girl?'

'How could you do this, Hazel? You know how I feel about men. I can't believe you did that.'

'Chill out, it's no big deal. He'll probably lose the number anyway.'

Mum and Dad were baby-sitting, so we stayed over at theirs. The next morning, Dad called me to the phone. 'A gentleman asking for you.'

'No, you deal with it,' I replied. 'We agreed you'd do the calls.'

'Somehow I doubt this caller is from Egypt,' Dad said with a wry smile.

I took the receiver from him.

'Hello?'

A quiet, confident and very English voice answered. 'Jacky? Hi, Ben here. How are you today?'

'Ben? Who the hell's Ben?' I replied rudely, knowing full well who it was.

'Recovering from half a lager and a packet of crisps?'

'What do you want?'

'Well, I was wondering. My parents have a caravan in the Yorkshire Dales. It's beautiful there. Would you like to spend the day with me?' As I sat dumbfounded, wondering what on earth to say, he added, 'Of course I meant you and the girls.'

That did it. I lost it. Even though he couldn't see me, I

stood up in anger. 'The girls? How in God's name do you know about them?'

Ben sounded taken aback. 'Sorry, have I said something I shouldn't have? Hazel said . . .'

He got no further. 'Oh, Hazel said, did she? Well, Hazel had no right. No, I don't wish to go to your caravan or anywhere else with you, whatever your name is. So don't bother ringing again. Goodbye.'

I slammed down the receiver. What a damned cheek! How dare he? How dare *she*, come to that. What was Hazel thinking of?

'So who was that then, J?' Dad came smiling into the hall. 'J' was his pet name for me. Funny, it was the first time he'd used it since our return.

'No one,' I answered hotly.

'Big reaction for a no one,' he murmured, walking away. He could be so infuriating sometimes.

7

Taking Control

We had been home for eighteen months. Even the letters from Egypt were slowing down. No one had attempted to snatch the girls. They were both happy in our little home. Leila was fast approaching eight and Amira three and a half. She now had a place at the nursery attached to the school where I was teaching. She spoke only English. With her green eyes and mop of curly, auburn hair, she looked and sounded English and fitted in extremely well. I had no idea how she felt about leaving Egypt, if she remembered or even understood what had gone on. So far, she hadn't asked where her daddy was, or why she didn't have one.

Leila was still very wary of strange men, and was upset when she moved up a year at school and discovered she would be having a male teacher. She developed rashes on her arms, neck and scalp. The doctor said it was stress-related, but I could go one further. It was Mr Bowman-related.

I had a quiet word, only mentioning how sensitive Leila was to change, and that she was very wary of people before she knew them. Would it be possible, I asked, to let her sit at the back, for him not to lean over to check her work, which would make her nervous, all that sort of thing. He was happy to oblige, and a few weeks later Leila decided that she quite liked Mr Bowman. The rashes disappeared in time for her eighth birthday party.

Life was on an even keel, but of course it didn't last. Omar wrote again, with the stark warning that I had forty days left to live.

I went straight to the police, who suggested they contact Omar and caution him. But it occurred to me that if we let them do that, he'd know his letters were getting through, and he'd begin bombarding us again with more lies and threats. Never replying was the one tactic which had worked to undermine his confidence. I decided against accepting help from the police, but I did inform the Home Office. They confirmed that they would not allow Omar into the country, although I knew this wouldn't stop him. I had been aware how easy it was for desperate, determined people to enter the UK illegally long before the immigration and asylum issues became subjects of hot debate. In Egypt, as everywhere in the Middle East, probably, it was a matter of routine to acquire a false passport by means of a bribe. Money talks in Egypt. Bribes make their world go round. Omar could do anything and we could do nothing. He made the rules.

Forty days passed. Nothing. Then another forty.

'I can't live like this.'

Mum and Dad had come over for Sunday dinner and the girls were in the garden.

'I mean, I'm so nervous all the time. I even chickened out of parents' evening, to avoid talking to the men. So now I'm not doing my job properly.'

'It's affecting us too, Jacky.' Mum's face was pale and drawn.

'I've come to a decision,' I said. 'If we carry on like this, then he's winning. Thousands of miles away, and he's still in control. From today, I'm going to live each day as if it were my last. I'm going to take control.'

I started going out again with Hazel, and saw Ben a few times across the room. He smiled each time and I found it easy to smile back. I began to feel guilty at the way I'd treated him. At a village dance in a huge marquee, I saw a chance to apologise.

The next thing I knew, we were dancing. When he kissed me, I kissed him back. He drove me home, but didn't come in. I gave him our new phone number and agreed to let him cook for me the following week. A proper date.

I'd picked up a second-hand bike for Leila and she was learning how to ride it. I spent ages running beside her and letting go, only to grab hold again. On the day of the date, I took the girls to Mum's, lugging the beloved bike with us on the bus. Mum made coffee, I put out paper and coloured pencils for Amira to draw and Leila went into the garden. Ten minutes later there was a terrifying scream.

Leila was lying at the bottom of the slope that ran from

the house to the garage. The bike was on top of her, the back wheel spinning furiously. Blood was trickling onto the concrete. She was not moving.

The ambulance men took a whole hour to examine her right there on the path with a blanket over her, before moving her into the ambulance and on to the hospital. She had managed to break her right arm and her left wrist, and needed twelve stitches above her eye where her glasses had smashed into her face. Sitting up in bed, she had one arm in plaster and one in a collar and cuff, unable to do anything for herself.

I spent the next fortnight at her bedside, feeding her, washing her and keeping her spirits up. She healed well and so did I. It helped me to see more clearly what was important. I remembered all the times I had bandaged her little arms or wrists, and bathed her face after brutal attacks from her angry father in Egypt. How we both knew we were powerless to stop him. How we both understood it would never stop.

Here in the hospital, Leila was surrounded by people who cared for her and wished her well. She would get better and go home to a peaceful, loving family. How lucky we were.

Poor Ben. Bombed out again. Not intentionally on my part, but he didn't know that. His calls were unanswered because there was no one at home. Amira stayed with Mum. Unsurprisingly, he gave up on me. While Leila was in hospital, I hadn't given him a second thought. Now she was home again, I realised with horror what I had done. Again.

I didn't have his number and spent a miserable week

worrying about it. Ben *was* a nice man and I'd been awful. Hazel had met someone new and was now seeing him, so my services as an escort weren't needed for the time being. I had no excuse to go out and no one to go out with. It just wasn't meant to be.

8

Moving On

I received a letter from a friend in Egypt, Nadine. She was an Essex girl, married to Hossein, an Egyptian business-man, and had been a very good friend to me out there.

'Come back, Jacky,' she wrote. 'Omar is so sad. He loves you so much. Better the devil you know.'

I gave the letter to Mum to file with the rest. I couldn't reply. He had charmed his way into their home and most likely urged her to write to me. She had no idea how he'd treated me.

I finally caught up with Ben in town, six months later. I was very humble and full of apologies. He stood there, letting me ramble on until I ran out of excuses. Then he just opened his arms and I leant into them. It felt great.

I arranged the first meeting between Leila, Amira and Ben in McDonald's. We kept it short, half an hour, extending the time at later meetings, until I asked him for tea at our home. Leila said nothing, but she wasn't rude. I prepared myself for the talk.

'What do you think of Ben, darling?'

'He's nice. Can I watch TV now?'

When we went walking in the woods, Leila slipped her hand into Ben's and they wandered off together in front. Within a month, he'd asked me to marry him.

'You'd better ask the girls,' I replied, tears coursing down my cheeks.

'Can we call you "Daddy"?' Amira asked.

'Yes, of course, silly. He's Daddy now.' Leila smiled up at Ben.

We married exactly one year later. The girls looked like fairies in their bridesmaid dresses and Mum and Dad were delighted. We snatched five days in the Lake District for our honeymoon, leaving the girls with them.

We returned to the biggest scare so far. Philomena and Richard, now living in Mum and Dad's old house, had received a visitor, looking for me. He was foreign and pretended that I had won some sort of competition. They had sent him away, but he had returned twice, which really unnerved Philomena.

I had taken Ben's surname, Trevane, when I married him. I was thirty-four and already I'd had five names! We changed the girls' names, again by Statutory Declaration. We decided to look around for a house a little further away, and explained that this would mean a change of schools for the girls. Neither of them realised we were moving around to make it more difficult to be found.

We moved. Bigger garden, family dog, car. I had everything I'd ever dreamed of, except that I knew how much Ben wanted another child. We discussed it long and hard, finally deciding to go for it. Three months later, we did it. The girls were excited. We began preparing for the new addition.

In Egypt I had lost four babies and kept two. For each one of those pregnancies, I had felt well and healthy. This time was different. I was ill, in pain and uncomfortable. Finally, it was discovered that it was a non-uterine pregnancy. The baby had somehow got through the cell wall into the stomach and would have to be aborted. We were devastated.

'Maybe I'm too old to have any more children? Maybe my body can't take any more after so many beatings and mis-carriages?'

'If you want to stop trying, that's okay with me.'

'No, Ben. We'll try again.'

'Look at what we have already. It's enough.'

In the end we decided to give it three months.

'What will be, will be,' said Ben.

I fell pregnant again during the third month. Adam was born a week before Christmas Day, a bouncing baby, weigh-ing six pounds. Our family was complete.

9

Empowerment

When we had first arrived back in England, it was with a one-year passport that I diligently renewed. When the law changed and every child had to have their own passport, I was unable to apply for Amira without her birth certificate. On the day of her birth, Omar's brother Mohamed had brought it into the hospital in Cairo, waving it around, saying, 'This is our insurance that you will never leave.'

This now became a problem. To obtain a passport for Amira, it was necessary to produce her birth certificate. Our local MP tried to locate the document anonymously, but to no avail. With a solicitor, I applied for and obtained British Citizenship for Amira and contacted the passport office. They were helpful and did a lot of groundwork on our behalf, but could not help us. The Court would not agree to us applying for a passport for her in our new surname.

'I think the best thing for you to do is wait,' said Carol, the lady at the passport office. 'When she's eighteen, she will no longer be a Ward of Court. She can legally change her surname by Deed Poll without her biological father knowing. Then she can apply for a passport in her own right.'

'But that's years away,' I replied, aghast.

'Better than rushing things now. If you apply in her real name, she could be traced.'

It was at this time that Amira mentioned Egypt, asking why Leila could have a passport and not her. I explained that Leila had been born in England, and therefore had a British birth certificate. We talked for about an hour about laws, nationality, officialdom, Egypt, but nothing directly about Omar. I let her lead the conversation, answering questions as fully as possible. She didn't ask anything personal to her or Omar, so I left it.

While they were growing up, neither Amira nor Leila mentioned their father, or their lives in Egypt. I could never understand how Amira could just blot out that part of her life unquestioningly. Years later, Leila revealed that she'd 'handled all that'. Obviously she'd done a good job, as Amira grew up into a well-balanced, competent young woman, who I'm extremely proud of. She can now talk freely to me about Omar, and has no desire to meet him or know anything more about him. Once again, Leila had been protecting me by handling all Amira's concerns confidentially.

I kept in touch with Carol over the years, and six months before Amira's eighteenth birthday, she advised me to make a fresh application. We sent everything off in good time, and on the eve of her birthday, Carol telephoned to say she had dispatched everything to be processed and it would be done first thing in the morning. She would post it on to us that same day.

'I'm opening a bottle of champagne to celebrate,' she informed me. 'It took fourteen years, but we've done it.'

This was the final hurdle. Amira receiving her long-awaited passport symbolised the end of our flight from Egypt. She was now a free, independent adult. A British citizen with a British passport in a British name. Finally, we had turned a corner and were free. Only the fatwa remained, which we would have to somehow incorporate into our lives and deal with. I had struggled to bring the girls up, but not without help and unconditional support of loved ones. There was Ben at my side, and I could not have managed without my parents. Now Mum was ill.

It happened suddenly. Mum went to the doctor's complaining of constipation, which had lasted a week. A scan revealed a massive invasion of cancer, covering all her major organs. She was in her early sixties, a non-smoker and active. Not overweight, she ate a healthy diet and had the odd glass of red wine. The prognosis was dire. Without treatment, two weeks; with treatment, longer.

It was as if the consultant was speaking in a foreign language. I struggled to take it in. He must have got the wrong person. Mum was going to live forever. She couldn't die. They'd definitely made a mistake.

My mother struggled on, fighting the disease for almost two years. She shouldn't have. Towards the end, she was in dreadful pain and suffered far too long. She was frightened to leave Dad on his own. I was close to finishing the book she had encouraged me to write, but didn't manage the final chapters before her death.

Ten weeks later, Dad caught a cold. It developed into a nasty chesty cough, and then into bronchial pneumonia. He was admitted into hospital. In a daze, I visited him and watched his body deteriorate. His kidneys collapsed. In intensive care he was put onto a ventilator. Fourteen days later, they switched him off. He lost his battle only twelve weeks after Mum.

It destroyed me. In my grief, I lost all reason, rejecting Ben's efforts to console me. Leila and Amira had both finished school and had left home to pursue their careers. I packed some clothes, took Adam, and left my husband.

We went to live in Mum and Dad's house. Somehow, by doing that, I thought I could cling on to them. I refused to speak to Ben. My life, as I knew it, was over.

It took six months for me to come to my senses, if that's what you'd call it. I knew I still loved Ben, but felt guilty being happy, when my parents had died so prematurely, seemingly without reason. It wasn't fair.

When Philomena phoned, it brought me back to reality with a bump. Omar had left yet another message on the answerphone. I couldn't handle it on my own. What the hell was I doing? Why had I left?

The message was for Leila. Omar left his number and asked her to speak to him. He said he had a lot of money that he wanted to transfer into her name and he needed her bank details. He would be coming to England soon and would go and see her nanna and grandad.

Philomena held me while I cried. 'Don't, Jacky, you're wearing yourself out,' she said. 'He knows only this address and we'll never tell.'

I wiped my eyes. My gaze fell upon the phone and the directory on the shelf next to it.

'Can I borrow the phone book for a minute, Philomena?'

Quickly, I found my father's surname. With my finger, I traced the name across to the address.

'What have I done? Omar's threatening to kill me. I get married, change my name, move away. Twice. Then throw it all away and move back to a house where even the dimmest dimwit could find me. Look.' I held the phone book out to Philomena. 'Dad's name, address and number. Very handy.'

* * *

That was a year ago. Why Ben gave me another chance, I'll never know. What I do know is that I'll never let him down again. Three months ago we moved into a different house, where Mum and Dad have never been. I've planted a cherry tree in the garden, and have photos and pieces of their furniture around. I will never get over their deaths, but I have now accepted that this new pain is another part of me.

Most of the time I feel free. I look over my shoulder every day; the fatwa is always in the background and I will always be wary. But I will not let it get in the way of me living my life to the full today and looking to the future with gratitude and hope.

Philomena and Richard still live in our old house. Omar continues to call. They never changed the number, as Richard works from home and it wouldn't be convenient. That's what they say, but like Carol at the passport office, Philomena and Richard are just being kind and protective. They know what a fatwa means and they know that if Omar keeps calling there, then he's not trying to call anywhere else. Technology has enabled Omar to make direct calls, which is how he managed to leave a message on Philomena's answerphone, although sometimes they still come through the operator. They often come on a Friday in the middle of the night.

It chills me to the bone, listening to *his* voice. He hasn't accepted that we don't live there. In Egypt among the lower classes, it is unusual to move house. Property is passed down through the generations. He actually speaks to the voice on the BT answer service as if it is Leila he is speaking to. It seems as if he's right there in the room with us. His voice has changed, aged, but through it I can see him as clearly as the day I left him sleeping in our bed in that flat in Cairo sixteen years ago.

He is the same man, unchanged. In contrast, I have changed. He made me invisible, hiding my real self beneath a blanket of submission.

I burned that blanket long ago.

*   *   *

The following chapters highlight the extent of other women's invisibility, in a variety of forms. Each chapter follows a different woman, as they tell me their stories. Every one is inspiring in its own right, yet shows us that invisible women are more common than we think.

10

Kareena: An Interview

'I'm getting married in three months, but not to my true love.'

That was pretty much all I knew about Kareena, but we'd agreed to meet up for her to tell me her story.

Sitting on the train, I closed my eyes and pictured Kareena in my mind. After so much soul-searching and endless emails, I was actually going to meet her face to face. Petite, I thought, with large, dark eyes and long hair. Dark, neutral clothes, or maybe even a sari of gentle, pastel colours. After all, it was summer.

The rain pelted onto the window as we hurtled towards the city. Typical British summer, but it did nothing to stem my excitement and anticipation.

'Oh my God! I've no idea what she really looks like.'

I sat up in alarm, opening my eyes to see all the surrounding passengers giving me strange looks.

'Sorry, must have been dreaming.' I excused myself hurriedly and began pondering this new problem. Why, oh why, hadn't I asked her what she'd be wearing, at the very least? I could be so stupid sometimes. Now what was I going to do? I'd never mentioned what I looked like. Leeds train station was massive. We'd never find each other.

As I rifled through my bag for any clue, I took out copies of the emails she had sent and saw her mobile number on the top one.

'Thank you, God,' I breathed, madly punching in the text message, 'What r u wearing? I'm in tan suede jacket and have umbrella.'

The reply took four long minutes to bleep its way through, 'White trousers.'

White trousers. That was the last thing I expected. A young, Pakistani Moslem girl, meeting me in white trousers. I realised how judgmental I had been in assuming she would be dressed demurely, to detract attention. Now I was more excited than ever to meet her.

'Clear your mind of everything, Jacky,' I told myself. 'Listen and learn.'

In fact, Kareena was the only girl standing on the platform wearing white trousers. She teamed them with a white T-shirt, a denim jacket and a wide smile. In her early twenties, her long black hair fell loosely around her shoulders, framing her face. As she smiled in welcome, she looked directly into my eyes and already I could sense a warmness between us. She led me to her car and we drove to a French bistro in the city centre for lunch and a chat.

On the way, Kareena chatted easily and confidently, asking me about myself and the journey. Once inside the bistro, we ordered lunch and she began to tell me her story:

'I was born in Bristol on 9 June. We only lived in Bristol for one year. Then my father's business moved to Wales, so we had to move there too. I have one older brother and two younger sisters. My sisters were both born in Wales. My parents both grew up in Pakistan. Dad came over in the 1950s. He was about fourteen at the time. Mum came over in the 1970s, after she got married to Dad. Mum never worked and Dad had his businesses. I was encouraged to work hard at school, went to college and gained a degree in Law. That was in Wales. I then came to the city to do a postgraduate degree.'

I couldn't help it. I had to interrupt. 'So if your parents allowed you to live alone in the city, they must be very liberal Moslems?'

Kareena nodded enthusiastically. 'Oh yeah, they're really cool in that sense. Because the thing about Pakistanis is, they have this weird set-up. They talk about being Moslem and following the ways of the religion, but a lot of it isn't Islam. It's their own little culture. You see, if you're Pakistani, you're born into a certain caste and they believe that you can only marry people who are Pakistani from the same caste. Now that's not Islam. That's their own interpretation. Islam says Moslem may marry Moslem. End of story. Which is fine. I can understand that. But I can't understand this other point of view. Take my auntie, for example. You would never believe, just by talking to her, that she'd been in Britain for the last thirty years. After all that time, she still has the same mentality that she came with. I always wear western clothes, but every time I leave the house, she frowns and disapproves. It really doesn't matter what clothes you wear, but the fuss she makes, honestly. And if my brother has to pour himself a glass of water, well, it's like there's a mini heart attack going on there. She thinks that's women's work.'

She paused and reached into her bag. 'Do you mind if I smoke?'

I shook my head, gazing at this feisty, independent, modern, intelligent woman in admiration. She seemed headstrong enough to cope with anything life found to throw at her. What was she going to tell me?

'But your parents remain supportive of your lifestyle?' I asked.

'Yes. My dad's very mature. But the other thing was, when we first came here they lived in a semi-detached house, which wasn't within the Pakistani community. They were quite isolated from the daily gatherings and goings-on that occur if there is a group living near to one another. So there was no one to gossip with. That's the thing. Pakistanis *love* to gossip. If you look at Pakistan today, it has actually moved on and the culture there is completely different to how they remember it. People come here and assume that Pakistan will always remain the Pakistan that they left. But in actual fact it has changed a lot.'

'How has it changed in respect of women, then?'

'People are just more liberal there now. Women are no longer chained to the sink or restricted to the house.'

'Have you spent much time out there?'

'When I was three we went for about six months, and we'd go back nearly every year after that for a month or so.'

'When you say that life has moved on, are you talking about the major cities, rather than the villages?'

'Life everywhere has moved on. Here, in the big semis in England, a lot of Pakistanis still don't send their children to school, especially the daughters. Yet in Pakistan now it is such a big thing. They must send their children to school. So people have come over here with their old values and implement them here, when they don't exist any more in their mother country. It's crazy.'

She put out her cigarette, shaking her head. 'It's like my little cousin. She's five years old and in a private school over in Pakistan, to give her the best opportunities. When my mother lived in Pakistan, there were no schools in the villages, but schools are popping up everywhere now. It's a big priority these days. I'm *so* glad my mum saw the value of education and let me study at university. We were all told, early on, that we *would* go to university, that we *would* work hard, that we *would* do something worthwhile with our lives. Even though Dad's businesses were successful, in the early years he had to really graft. So his attitude is, why should we, his children, have to go through that?'

'So tell me about your siblings. Have they all done well for themselves?'

'My brother's an accountant. My sister went to university to study medicine, but decided it wasn't for her and she is now studying for a degree in journalism. Things are really different for my little sister, though. She was really ill when she was a baby *and* she's the youngest, the baby of the family. My parents have been very lenient with her as a result. She's started so many things and not finished them. She started A levels. Then she gave them up and started a hair and beauty course for a bit. That didn't work out, and she got a part-time job as a care assistant in a nursing home. This looks as if it will work out. She's enjoying it. She really cares. So next year she'll try to get into nursing. The point is, my parents let her pursue whatever interested her. They gave her that freedom. Not like us.'

The background music in the bistro, at first pleasing and atmospheric, was now an interference and highly irritating. I leaned forward, engrossed, eager to hear every word of Kareena's story.

'I get on well with my parents and my siblings. My dad was very affectionate. When we were kids he was always hugging and kissing us.'

She paused, then added, 'Even now, really.'

I wanted to know more. 'What's your dad like?'

Kareena smiled as she described him. 'Actually, he's quite young-looking for his age. In fact he's sixty-three, but looks and acts much younger. He's tall and slim. He smokes, not too heavily, unless he is angry or tense. Then he drinks gallons of coffee and smokes like a chimney, so we know when to give him space. But usually he is a calm person with a love of sports cars. I'd describe him as quiet, yet with a strong sense of presence.'

'Sounds like a formidable character. So tell me about you and this independent life of yours. How did this go down with your father?'

When I left home to come and live here, I got a place in halls for a year. Then my dad rented a house here, as he had quite a bit of business in the city, and I moved there. He stays a couple of nights a week. The other thing about this city is, most of the Pakistanis are from Kashmir, which is like a thousand years behind everyone else, complete traditionalists. We, as a family, are much more forward-thinking. I was the first girl in our entire family to go to university, and in the community where the family lives now, I was the first girl to get a part-time job. Ten, fifteen years ago, this would never have been allowed. The pressure would have been too much, even for my parents.'

'Okay, Miss Modern-Day Pakistan, tell me about boy-friends. How far does this liberal attitude stretch?'

Kareena smiled. 'Technically, I've never had one. In reality I was a normal teenager. You know the sort of thing, first crush at school; you see him now and think, "What a geek." As we do. Kevin, that was his name. But we never actually went out. I didn't really go out with anyone until I went to college. He was a Saudi and he was okay, but nothing serious. I had my first serious relationship at twenty-one, with a guy from Rochdale. We met through his cousin who was a friend of mine. I thought the world of him, but he was a lad's lad, you know, getting drunk every weekend. He was a Pakistani, but he let me down a lot. My dad never knew about him, but my sister knew. Eventually he dumped me. I was completely devastated. I thought it was love at the time, but looking back I don't think it was, as we were so nasty to each other most of the time. Anyway, I needed time out. I was working for Immigration Control by then and applied for an exchange. I was accepted and was sent to Waterloo, which meant three days in London and two days in France, at the Gare du Nord in Paris. I can't speak a word of French. It was two years ago now.

'Anyway, I went down to London, met new friends and got on very well with them, going out a lot and socialising until I was able to relax and start feeling better about myself. Even the early morning starts didn't seem so bad.

'I met Salah by making a fool of myself trying to order coffee in French, when it turned out he spoke perfect English. We had a laugh and there was this instant attraction. I bought so many coffees, I had to give them away, but it was worth it to chat to him. He got the message in the end. He really set my heart on fire. But I daren't ask him out. In the end, my friend marched up to him and asked him if he'd take me out to dinner. Everyone heard, Customs and Excise, Immigration Officers, French Immigration Officers and Eurostar staff. It was so embarrassing. He looked over, smiled and said, "Okay". And that was that.

'We went out for dinner, our first date, and he was late. Not good. He got stuck on the tube. But he was definitely worth the wait. From the start it was as if we were old friends catching up. We had so much in common, so much to laugh about. I had the best time. He was a Moslem, from Morocco. And he was gorgeous. In the blink of an eye it was one o'clock in the morning and we were still sitting in the restaurant, engrossed in each other's company.'

I smiled. 'So he was worth the initial embarrassment then?'

'Definitely. I'd do it all over again. After that we saw each other as much as possible. We were perfect for one another. I fell in love and so did he. I was so happy. But my time was soon up and I was posted back to the Midlands and away from Salah. A couple of months later, having only spoken on the phone, he said, "What are we going to do? I can't bear to be apart from you." He proposed and I thought my heart would burst. I couldn't wait to be his wife.'

I leaned backwards to let the waiter clear the table. 'But that's brilliant, Kareena. I was expecting a tragic end to this tale. It's pure romance: see dark, handsome stranger across a crowded café, arrange a date, hit it off straightaway, dream of each other night and day, marriage proposal, proposal accepted. And the wedding's in three months?'

Kareena lit another cigarette. 'Yes. No. Not quite. I mean . . . let me tell you exactly what happened. We agreed that the next step was for me to tell my parents all about us and that we wished to marry. This was the difficult part. I couldn't just come out with it. It actually took me about a month to broach the subject. I gradually built up to it, bringing things up in conversation, like who we can and can't marry, things like that. I got the response, "Well, it

65

doesn't really matter but, you know our society. We have our culture to consider, and we only marry Pakistanis. You will have to marry from the same caste." That sort of thing. One of my married cousins snorted in disbelief and said what a lot of rubbish he thought of that, but mostly the family still held the traditionalist view. It was important for me to get to know their feelings about the subject before I jumped in with both feet. All this scared me, so I kept putting it off. Salah kept trying to reassure me that there was nothing wrong with what we wanted to do. He urged me to just come out with it and tell my parents once and for all. "But you must stick to your guns," he kept saying.

'I was in a dilemma. Should I tell my mother first? Maybe it would be better to tell my father? Or should I take the bull by the horns and tell them both together? I dilly-dallied for another couple of weeks, until I just blurted it out to my father one day, surprising even myself.

' "Dad, I've met someone, a boy, who I really like, and I'd like you to meet him. He works mainly in France, and we met when I was doing that stint down south for Immigration."

'I waited with baited breath. He stopped what he was doing, looked at me and gave his answer, "No".

'No discussion. Nothing. I tried to reason with him. I asked him to hear me out, but he put up his hand and started ranting and raving, ending with the chilling words, "You have no choice about this. Forget him. Now."

'This was a year ago. I told him that as far as I was

concerned I had done nothing wrong and it was a reasonable request, but he would have none of it. We didn't speak again for six months.

'My mum tried to make me see that he was not good enough for me, calling him uneducated, when she didn't know anything about him. I soon put her straight. Salah had a first-class honours degree and was very "educated", thank you. He wasn't an idiot, merely working part-time in a café. Mum said they had to arrange a marriage for me, from my own caste. That did it. We had a huge row.

' "How come we were all told when we were young we had to work hard and do well for ourselves, but no one mentioned that we'd have to marry who *you* say?" I screamed at her. "How could you forget such a major thing as that? You're such hypocrites. Pick and choose religion and culture when it suits. You're obviously more concerned with what this looks like to other people than how your daughter feels. This is not how we've been brought up. It's not my culture. It's your culture. It's not fair. And it's just not good enough." I collapsed on the settee, sobbing.

' "Just because you have a British passport doesn't make you British," she replied.

' "That's just splitting hairs," I retorted.

'But it was no use. Salah just could not believe it. "I've never heard of anything so ridiculous in my life," he told me. Unless you're a Pakistani, you'll never really understand their ways.

'Salah never did get to meet my father. If he had, my

father would have killed him. It was that serious. I had to decide what to do next. My cousin sat me down and gave me his opinion.

' "Listen, Kareena. Your parents are never going to accept this. Never. This leaves you with two choices. You can finish things with Salah, forget about him and move on, or you can go upstairs right now, pack your bags and leave. Make a life with Salah and then afterwards do what you can to build bridges with your parents. It's up to you."

'Salah told me to choose, but said I had to be quite sure of what I wanted and what it would mean, never seeing my family again. I knew, if I chose that path, there would be stressful times ahead. My father would come after me and all hell would break loose. What would he do to me, if pushed to the limit?

'I'm a very soft-hearted person. If I left it would cause chaos. I didn't have it in me to do that. It's the way I am. Yeah, I loved him more than life itself, *but* it would have meant putting my mum through absolute hell. I made my decision and never saw Salah again. I was posted to a different airport for two months, which gave me little time to think about what I'd done.

'In the meantime, my mother had registered me with the meat market. She circulates my details around the corners of the Pakistani community at home and abroad and waits for the suitors to come knocking. Nothing to do with who you really are and what you've achieved in your life. All that matters is, "is she tall enough, is she skinny enough, is she beautiful enough?" It's so primitive, and worse, it's my life she's playing with. Like, after five minutes of clapping eyes on some bloke, it's, "yes, I want to marry him". As if!

'I came back to a number of "appointments". Dressed up like a blinking Christmas tree. I ask you. Sitting in the front room, waiting to be looked over. And not just by the bloke. All the relatives push in to have a look and give their two-pennorth. Mum hit the jackpot after six. To a large extent it was her choice rather than mine. Obviously if I'd really detested him, she would have declined, but I'd reached the point of acceptance by then, and he was the best of them all. The first five were total geeks. I mean, a lot of them lie. Like they say they're a doctor, but they're still studying. Mum rings the agent – not really an agent, just some woman sitting in her front room – to find out if they are who they say they are. It all started like that. "Oh hello, I need to get my son married now, can you arrange it?" and a few months down the line it's sorted. It's a large network they've got going.

'My "betrothed" is Pakistani in origin, but has spent years in Europe studying. All his brothers and sisters have been educated in Europe too. At present he's working in a hospital in London. I actually said to my Mum, "I'm past caring. If you like him, go ahead. Do what you have to do, I really don't care." So they did, and in three months I'll be a married woman.'

I was shocked. 'It seems a bit of a whirlwind marriage. Are the parents pushing you together to see more of each other before your big day?'

'Not really. He works full-time. So far we've met only twice. We talk on the phone. To be fair, he's a nice guy . . .'

'But?'

'But, he's not Salah.' She sighed, lost in thought. 'There's the age thing as well, I suppose. Of course, there are still girls who marry at sixteen and have three kids by the age of twenty. It depends what sort of family you come from. But increasingly, as education is becoming more of a priority for daughters as well as sons, marriage occurs later and later. I have an auntie who is pursuing her career at thirty and is still not married. A few years ago she would have been pressurised to give it up to marry, or face life as a single woman and basically an outcast. Now it's just not like that. She'll probably marry when she's ready and have a happy life, accepted by the community.'

'So it hasn't occurred to you to run away on the eve of your wedding, then?'

She shook her head firmly. 'No, nothing like that. I couldn't do it to my family.' She looked down sadly. 'It's my choice. I've resigned myself to my fate.'

'Where will you live?'

She smiled and I caught a glimmer of the Kareena I had met only hours ago, happy to meet me, free. 'At least that's in my hands. He's a doctor. Work isn't a problem, he can work anywhere. So he'll go anywhere. He's much keener on this alliance than I am, so that's one good thing.'

'Do you think you'll be able to break the chain with him?

70

I mean, will you allow your children to marry any other Moslem regardless of race or caste?'

'That's one of my dreams. I can only hope. He's a modern guy who's spent most of his life in Europe. Maybe it will be possible. Who knows? It will all depend on my new husband. He may stay as he is, liberal and westernised, or he could revert and become more traditional once we are married. I hope he doesn't. The future could be very stressful. I can be really stroppy when I get going. There could be a bumpy ride ahead.'

I had a lump in my throat as I stood on the platform, watching Kareena return to her car. I was filled with admiration for her strength of character and resolve. I marvelled at the selfless love she had for her family, and yet I felt a sadness, that she was taking the first steps of that fateful journey. The journey that began with resignation, entered into submission along the way, until she reached the inevitable destination: invisibility.

Kareena, may you be at peace in your future life. I wish you every happiness and all the luck in the world. Break the mould and be yourself. Go, girl!

11

Laura

I sat cross-legged on our living-room sofa, enjoying morning coffee with my friend Laura. Gregarious, funny, spirited Laura. I'd actually known her for around ten years. I'd taught her son at school and Laura had always been one of the proactive parents, helping in the classroom, walking with us down to the swimming baths every week, forever encouraging her children in whatever they chose to pursue. In fact her sunny smile had a positive effect on us all in the school and we became firm friends.

Friendship. Every one is different, yet we all know what we mean when we say the word. In our case, we chatted about the kids, our partners and our daily niggles and put the world to rights. The years passed and eventually her two children left the safe environment of the primary school for the much larger, scarier world of bigger kids, lots of classrooms and a cafeteria where you chose and paid for your own dinner.

I too decided to make the transition from primary to secondary teaching, and as a result Laura and I lost touch for a while. We'd bump into each other in town occasionally, promising to get in touch and not managing it. Life somehow got in the way. Until the day she read *Fatwa. Living with a Death Threat.*

'I'm not used to this.' Laura drained the last of her coffee. 'I mean, it's something I've made such an effort to conceal over the years. Only Ian understands.'

Ian was her husband and her rock; solid, supportive and calm. They had presented a united front as a family through all their problems over the years, while friends around them divorced, remarried or had affairs.

'I come from a large family, but as far as they are concerned, I might just as well be dead. It's been like that since I was eight years old. Ever since then. It's as if I don't exist.'

I stared at her. How on earth can you be friends for ten years with someone and not be aware of a trauma such as this? Very easily, obviously. And if your friends hide their afflictions so well, what about all the other women walking around with a cheery smile on their face? There must be 'invisible women' everywhere.

'I could be in your book,' she continued. 'I'm not foreign or religious or even in a troubled marriage. But I'm invisible, nevertheless.'

She continued talking and I asked if she'd mind if I recorded what she was saying. She merely shrugged. Laura always wants to please.

'My early childhood memories are happy ones, full of love and laughter, surrounded by my family. I had a very loving mum. I had a twin brother, Matt, but my best friend was my older sister, Jane. We did everything together, even wore the same clothes but in different colours.'

'What was the difference in age between you two?'

'She was just two years older than me and we adored each other. I still have old cine films of us growing up, of her always holding my hand, always beside me, always looking after me.'

'Do you have a special memory about the family, when you were all together?'

'I remember sitting on the settee and watching *Watch with Mother*, at dinner-time. I also have a brother Rob, who's four years younger. We all used to come home at dinner-time and sit watching the telly. I remember snuggling up to Mum and looking up at her, smelling her, inhaling all her scent. Just the warmth of having a mum. And I grew up in an ideal world.'

'Was Dad around?'

'Yes, he worked down at the docks. We had countless good times together. He always made sure we had two holidays each year at Butlin's. I know that might not sound much, but when you're a kid you don't need much. It was just bliss. Everything I ever wanted.'

I was fascinated. A loving family with brothers and sisters. I'd always dreamed of having a twin brother myself. 'Did you get on with your twin?'

'Yes. In fact we still do, to a certain degree. But then, growing up, we always had time for each other, always playing. Even after . . .' she trailed off.

I leant forward and poured more coffee from the pot. The smell of ground coffee beans wafted around us. 'So what changed everything?'

Laura, lost in her thoughts, looked up at me sadly. 'I didn't know then and I don't know now.'

It was impossible to hazard a guess as to what major event had taken place to change her life forever. 'So was it instant, this change, or gradual?'

'To me it was instant. I mean at eight I wasn't aware of time or space or anything. My whole world was the there-and-then. I didn't think of yesterday, tomorrow or last week. I just lived day by day. But that day will haunt me forever. It was a Sunday. I came downstairs in the morning and went into the dining-room at the back of the house to find every item of Jane's clothing hanging up on the picture-rail all around the room. And by 'everything', I mean, everything. She had a cape, all her skirts, T-shirts and dresses. All her toys as well. I remember the pile of her dolls and teddies. Everything.'

'Did she share a room with you then?'

'Yes. Anyway, Mum followed me into the room and simply said, "These belong to you now. Jane doesn't need them any more." I had no idea what was happening. No further explanations were offered. I had to put up and shut up. I never did wear any of those clothes, because that whole day signified the end of the relationship between me and my beloved sister. Literally, one minute I had a sister, and the next, nothing. No one would have been able to persuade me to touch any of her things after that day.'

I was confused. 'I don't understand. Did Jane change towards you after that day?'

'Totally. Overnight she became a tomboy, disinterested in me, never playing with me. Her personality changed. To me, it literally seemed instantaneous.'

'Did her attitude change towards other people, or just towards you?'

'To me.' Laura nodded meaningfully. 'Definitely towards me. Suddenly I was the little sister she no longer wanted. Mum suddenly didn't want her ten-year-old daughter any longer, so Jane was reinvented and her 'girlie' clothes and toys were pushed onto me. I certainly had no choice in any of it. The irony was that I was used to wearing Jane's clothes, as she often passed them down to me. Which was fine. But this!'

Laura leaned forward and put her face in her hands. 'This was different. It was as if Jane had died. A complete clear-out of the bedroom. It wasn't right. Mum said she wouldn't buy me any more clothes until I had outgrown all of those. And she stuck by her guns. Such a horrible thing. And no one would explain why.'

'But Laura, that was thirty years ago. Surely you know now?'

Laura shook her head. 'Jane and Mum are very alike. Both hate fuss, very no-nonsense, spartan. Physically, Jane is not feminine in any sense of the word. She doesn't have any boyfriends or any relationships at all. She lives on her own, no social life, just sits alone in the house under a pile of blankets, with the heating switched off. She's very much a loner. Every time we meet she hurls abuse at me, finding fault with anything and everything. I still make the effort every year and go round to Mum and Dad's at Christmas with Ian and the kids, which we enjoy doing, but even then Jane will be nasty to me if she feels like it. At my niece's birthday party, Jane made a vicious comment about me in front of thirty people, loud enough for them to hear her clearly, and making sure that Ian was in the vicinity. She just doesn't care. She thinks it's funny. Sly little digs. She's very manipulative. She seems to have taken up the cause; where Mum attacks mentally, Jane is more physical, more vocal. Both are spiteful and neither are able to show emotion in the normal sense of the word.'

I wondered at the power of siblings over other siblings. Surely Laura had found a way over the years of facing up to Jane. Her story stirred up a lot of emotions inside me, making me want to confront this family myself and sort it out once and for all. But I voiced none of my feelings. Instead, I asked, 'How do you deal with that now?'

'Over the years, I've learnt to ignore it. I don't have the confidence to stand up to her. I never will have. But that's how I feel about my whole family. Jane's a bully, and so are all the rest of them. I've tried to ask them what happened when I was eight, but every time I am fobbed off with, "Don't talk about that time. It was all *your* fault. You were far too troublesome. Now don't raise the subject again." '

'How frustrating. Pretty scary, too, for an eight-year-old?'

'I was terrified. Jane had been my other half. Now she refused to play with me or let me touch any of her things. I remember wanting to clean the bedroom once and Jane wouldn't let me. When I called Mum, Jane shoved me so hard in the back that I fell all the way down twelve steps onto a concrete floor. She used to get angry and lose it. Once she stabbed me in the leg with a pencil for nothing. If a friend came over, she would never share a game or let me join in. She just saw it as another opportunity to push me away. Matt used to play with me sometimes. Usually he was fine on his own. Jane would leave us alone to play. She'd never join in. Then she'd say something to him, and he would leave me and side with her. If we ever argued, she'd interrupt and take Matt away. I spent more and more time on my own. My confidence and sense of security completely disappeared, until I began to blame myself. Maybe all this *was* my fault after all. If I got no attention for being good and quiet, then would I get any for being defiant and loud? So I tried it. Bad idea.'

'Why?'

'I ended up, at the age of eight, sitting in a psychiatrist's office. I mean, imagine the trauma of having to be taken out of lessons at school to see the psychiatrist. They weren't very sensitive at school in those days. Everyone knew and I was so ashamed.' Laura paused to wipe a tear from the side of her cheek. 'It turned out that my mum and dad blamed me for everything. They said they couldn't control me. They talked about me as if I was some sort of wild animal. It's bizarre. I can remember that office as if it were only yesterday. One of the first times I went there, I saw a Mrs Morton, who gave me some paper and told me to draw a picture of my family. It took me ages. The finished picture showed me and Dad. That was it. Yet Dad was one of the abusers too. I don't know why I drew him. But to me, that was my family.'

'Was this a family therapy session, or was it just for you?'

'Oh, just for me. My mum took me. She used to sit in an outer room, observing me through a one-way mirror, although she couldn't hear what was going on. The funny thing was, as humiliating as it was to be taken out of class to go there, once there, I really got involved with the sessions. I grew to love it because, as hard as it was, it was *my* time. I remember, during one visit, my brothers and sister were brought into the room to play with me. I went mad. I was furious. They were in *my* space, touching *my* toys. This was my refuge, the only place where I had the chance to be me without being punished for it, and suddenly my siblings barged in and took this away. I wanted to be left alone to play in peace, something that had stopped on that fateful day.'

'What do you mean?'

'At home, Jane would disrupt everything, taunting me and encouraging Matt to join in and, later, Rob. Verbal and physical. It never stopped. Blame always came to rest at my door, whatever the others did. The others had friends. I was the only one not allowed to bring friends round. One evening both Matt and Jane were holding me down and bouncing up and down on my chest. I couldn't breathe. Mum and Dad just sat there and watched it happen. I got told off and sent upstairs for antagonising them! They found excuses to give me a beating five or six nights a week. It got so ridiculous that I'd get hit for wearing the wrong coloured T-shirt or accidentally spilling a drink. And it wasn't a slap. Proper hitting, I can tell you, followed by banishment to my room. I was the one the family didn't like. The burden.'

I could feel myself becoming more and more angry as she spoke about being beaten. Why had all this happened? What excuse could an adult come up with for continually resorting to beating an eight-year-old girl? 'Did you ever get hit before you were eight?' I asked.

'That's the thing. Not once. Would you believe it?' She hung her head. 'I can't help thinking sometimes, that ultimately I might have helped them be horrible to me. Because I was naughty after everything changed and I was suddenly pushed out into the cold. I just gave them the excuse they needed to exclude me even more.'

'But why would they want to exclude you in the first place?'

'I really wish I knew. Dad gave me mixed messages all the time. I was so confused. It's making me shiver now, thinking of all the times they abused me. Most nights, Dad would take me upstairs and literally punch me until I had rolled myself into a tight ball on the floor. He would then leave me sobbing and stand outside the door for as long as it took for me to stop. Whereupon he would come back in, put his arm around me and tell me it was for the best. I spent every night alone. I used to pray that someday someone would notice me. It makes my stomach turn when I recall how I used to feel.'

I jumped up to sit beside Laura. My stomach wasn't feeling so good either, so it must have been taking a lot for her to tell me everything so candidly. 'How else did they abuse you?'

Laura linked her fingers together, clenching her hands tightly. 'Where do I start? I would get pulled by my hair all the way upstairs from the bottom step. I would go to school with bald patches in my scalp. It was always Dad. Mum concentrated on the mental abuse, putting me down, sneering, leaving me out, giving me "the look", until I left the room. Dad did the physical stuff.'

'Can you give me an example of what you had to do to warrant a beating?' I asked gently. 'Only if you want to,' I added quickly.

Laura smiled wryly. 'How many do you want? Always little things, like colouring on my brother's book. That time I was dragged off the book by my hair and told to get out of the room.

'And if he coloured on your book?'

'Oh, that was different. Mum and Dad would reason with them and sort things out. It was okay for the others to lock me in the garden shed for hours on end. It was okay for Jane to touch anyone's things. But not me. When she stabbed me in the leg with her pencil, so hard that it stayed upright, she didn't get told off at all. Instead, I got a beating for annoying her. And if I tried to stand up to them, they couldn't handle it, so things became even worse. Once I refused to leave the room, saying, "It's not fair." Dad wrenched me up from the ground and I clung to the door on the way out. As he dragged and punched me up the stairs, I reacted by lashing back at him. He was furious. He swung me into the bedroom by my hair. I flew into the room, landed heavily on my elbow and ended up in hospital.'

I felt an enormous sense of relief. Her dad had beaten her once too often and now the doctors would inform the authorities to put a stop to the abuse. I couldn't wait for Laura to tell me. 'So then people at the hospital started asking questions?' I asked eagerly.

'You have to remember, this was around 1970. Hospitals never looked into anything like that then. It was a wonder, considering all the bruises I had. At first, no one bothered when I said my elbow hurt. I remember lying in bed that night in so much pain that I crept from my room into Dad's to get a scarf to wrap it up with. I almost wet myself with fear in case anyone heard me coming out of my room, but my elbow was throbbing so badly, I had to risk it. But no one heard me. They were all watching telly downstairs. It wasn't until I went down the next morning with a very swollen elbow, that Mum took any notice. She took one look at it from across the kitchen, sighed and told Dad he'd better take me to hospital, seeing as he was the one who had done it. Then she turned back to the sink. Not an ounce of sympathy, compassion or concern. Like I said before, this was Mum's method of abuse.'

I was dumbfounded. Nothing. How could they do nothing? 'Was there anyone else you could talk to?'

'Eventually I started going to my grandma and grandad's after school for a bit. They only lived at the end of the road. They were nice to me.'

'Thank the Lord. Did you ever ask them anything about what might have happened?'

Laura shook her head. 'I didn't dare. Quite simply, it was never spoken of. Not then. Not now. To this day, I'm not sure who in the rest of the family knows about it. Certainly no one has ever mentioned anything to me. When I was younger, it occurred to me to ask aunties and uncles. But I was never sure what Mum might have said and I was scared. So the questions were never asked. I just couldn't trust anyone. I always had this dream of running away to live with family friends, but I couldn't trust my mum. It wasn't until last year that I discovered from a neighbour that the whole street had been aware of what was going on. I was absolutely stunned that not one single person thought it appropriate to intervene. I was left to suffer and they'd known all along.'

'It was a lot for a little girl to cope with.'

'I was just a little girl who wanted her family back and had no idea what to do to get it. The trouble was, I just wasn't . . .' She hesitated and began to cry as she finished the sentence, '. . . wanted.'

I put my arm around her and hugged her close. It was several minutes before Laura felt ready to carry on.

'I remember Jane wanting to leave home, after an argument with Mum. I can't remember the reason, but I do remember Mum stopping her at the door and talking her out of it. It was different with me. I must have been about ten. I'd had enough of the fighting, shouting and bullying, so I packed my little suitcase to leave, all the while not really wanting to go. In hindsight, I can see this was a cry for help, for someone to show they cared, or loved me enough to make me stay. In one way I wanted to stay, in another I couldn't bear another minute in that house. Of course, I'd seen Jane go through the same motions. I'd seen Mum hurriedly block the door and talk her out of it. Now it was my turn. Heart beating loudly, I approached the front door, having told Mum I was leaving. No one rushed in to stop me. No one cared. So, at ten years old, I opened that front door and walked right out of it and down the street with my little suitcase. With every step I took, I was praying for someone to run into the street and call out my name. I would have smiled my widest smile and skipped back in happily and said sorry for leaving. But I never got the chance. I got to the end of the street before it dawned on me that no one was ever going to call out my name or follow me. I hadn't planned what to do after that. This wasn't what was supposed to have happened. I wanted to burst into tears there and then. But I made my face calm, as if I wasn't bothered, turned around and headed back to the house, through the front door and upstairs to my bedroom. No one looked for me, no one even mentioned me going. It was a total non-event as far as the rest of the family was concerned. When Mum finally noticed that I had returned, nothing was said. She didn't care. I threw myself onto my bed and sobbed and sobbed. I'd never felt so alone, so unwanted, so unloved.'

I nodded sympathetically. 'I can identify with those feelings, although I was a grown woman when it happened to me,' I said. 'In Egypt, I had a few friends at the school where I taught, with whom I could let off steam sometimes. It made me feel a whole lot better. Did you manage to escape at school?'

Laura smiled ruefully. 'That would have been great, wouldn't it? I honestly think I would have come through things much better if I'd had a great time at school. But it just didn't happen. I was bullied all the way through school too. Mum refused to buy me new clothes, so I was picked on for that. I was in second-hand clothes until the day I could pay for something new from my pay packet from work. It was totally humiliating. I had absolutely no one to talk to. I couldn't tell the teachers, because they'd tell my parents, who would just take it out on me more at home. I lived in fear of kids at school and my parents at home. Sometimes I had to choose between them. Once I had to take money from Mum's purse and risk the consequences, to pay the bullies at school not to hurt me. One day, at secondary school, Mum brought in some Wellington boots for me to change into. They actually put a message out over the Tannoy for me to go to the office and change. She told the staff that my shoes were wet. They weren't. For some reason she wanted to humiliate me further. It worked. I was bullied all day, even worse than usual. And then there was the school photo. The school uniform had changed when I was fourteen. On the day of the school photo, when I was sixteen, she made me squeeze into my old uniform. I was the only pupil, out of a thousand, in that photo who was wearing the old uniform, and to top it all I was bursting out of it all over. I stood out like a sore thumb. The other pupils had a field day. No, school was a terrible time for me.'

She leant forward to look into the coffee pot. 'Any chance of another?'

It was stone cold. 'How about a glass of wine?' I suggested. 'I don't know about you, but I could certainly do with one, and there's one with our names on it in the fridge.'

'Go on then, Jacky. You've twisted my arm.'

She laughed, as I returned in record time with two large glasses of chilled Chardonnay.

'How long did you see the psychiatrist for?' I asked.

'I saw the psychiatrist for over a year. He helped a lot, I suppose, but Ian has been my saviour. Ian's amazing, you know.' She took a large gulp of wine. 'He's gone over and over everything with me. He pointed out that Mum never went to see anyone to talk to. Maybe something did happen and Mum could not bring herself to confront it and talk about it. When everything changed for me, it wasn't just Jane who stopped wearing girlie clothes. Mum also lost her femininity. She wore slacks instead of dresses, in fact she wore slacks with a T-shirt and a cardigan every day. She has worn the same style ever since. She was a loving, caring mother who changed into a cold, emotionless woman, who didn't want me for a daughter any longer. So I became the scapegoat. I mean, what is it that an eight-year-old can do that is so major as to cause such disruption and warrants all that abuse and neglect? It just doesn't make sense. It's also very hard to accept that you can get hurt so much in life as a consequence of your parents' actions. It really cuts deep. I'm shaking inside but, at the same time, it's good to talk, and be listened to.'

I felt humble, sitting there, listening to my friend spill out such emotion and anguish. In that moment, I didn't feel like a very good friend at all. 'It's easy to listen,' I replied. 'But I'm not sure how I can help.'

Laura smiled. 'You're helping already, just by sitting there, letting me offload it all. I feel a lot better already. Sometimes I think I'm going mad with only Ian who understands. He has lots of theories. He thinks that maybe Mum's reason for changing was transferred onto Jane to protect her in some way. In giving me all Jane's girlie clothes, maybe I reminded her of what she was trying to erase from her life. So she rejected me. It was easier to push me away, than to sort out her problem. Was being feminine a threat in some way to Mum?'

'It's obviously had a big effect on the person you are today,' I said.

'In lots of ways. Like the telephone. Even now, I'm nervous about using it. It was used as a weapon, you see. Sometimes I would dare to creep halfway down the stairs to sit and listen to the noises the rest of the family were making; the low rumble of conversation, the hum of the telly, the occasional laughter. I would imagine myself sitting happily in the room with them, all warm and cosy. Sometimes, Dad would come out and catch me. He would immediately pick up the phone and pretend to contact the children's home. It makes me feel really ashamed that at the age of nine or ten, I would throw myself at his feet and plead and beg my own father not to send me away. And all he ever did was to shout, "You've done it this time. You're going. We don't want you here. We want a family, and that doesn't include you." It's a pitiful thing to see a child beg. It really is. I can see in my mind what I used to be like and I'm ashamed of it. This could happen several times a week, but I still believed that if he got through on that telephone, I would be sent away.'

'What if you misbehaved in the daytime? Were you still dragged upstairs?'

'No. Daytimes were different. I'd do something trivial, and be thrown out of the house. It wouldn't matter what I was wearing, or what the weather was like. I might just have a vest and a pair of knickers on and be thrown out into the front garden. They'd lock the door, so I'd run round to the back as quickly as I could. I've since realised it was a cruel game. The whole family, even little Rob, would race to the back door. When I got there, Mum would calmly turn the key to lock the door and they would all stand there pointing and laughing at me. I would then go back to the front and stand at the front window and watch them, until Jane came over to draw the curtains and shut me out of their lives. They usually made me stand out there for about half an hour, even if it was blowing a gale and pouring with rain and I had no shoes or socks on. I'd curl myself up on the concrete step and wait miserably. When they eventually let me in, Dad would drag me in by my hair and throw me upstairs to bed.'

'So you were never with them really?'

'No.'

'Who did you get on with the most?'

'Matt, my twin, I suppose. Jane made sure that she kept Rob well away from me. She would make sure she sat next to him, played with him. I never got the chance to play with him. The only time I can remember is one year going on holiday, we had to do the halfway changeover in the car, where the two in the middle seats swapped with the two on the outside. This one time, Rob ended up next to me and he fell asleep on my shoulder. I was on top of the world. My little brother was close to me, even if just for a short time.'

'So after the age of eight, even though you lived within a family of six, you virtually grew up alone?'

'I learnt how to be on my own, to play by myself. I couldn't see why this was happening, and I retreated into my own little world. And in that world, I was happy. That was how I lived. Seventeen years ago, my cousin got married. I was married to Ian at the time and we had moved to Bristol. We came over to Mum's to travel up to Liverpool with her, where the wedding was. Mum was in a foul mood, I don't know why. Anyway, she reverted to norm and, in front of Ian, took it out on me. We'd just had our first baby, Jack, who was six months old, and he started crying. It gave me the confidence I needed to confront Mum. I asked her, there and then, exactly what it was that I'd done that was so bad. She looked me right in the eyes and said coldly, "I'll never tell you. But I will say this. Till the day I die I will never forgive you for what you did to this family." Then she just walked away and left me. Seventeen years on, she still hasn't told me what it was.'

'That's a pretty large burden to carry around.'

'Ian thinks I should go to a hypnotist to see if I can remember anything that way. I am thinking about it.'

'So how did Ian come into the picture?'

'Well, I left school at sixteen and started work straightaway. I had to prove to myself that I didn't need my family. At school, I'd done some work experience in a hospital. I absolutely loved it, and came home knowing I wanted to go into nursing. My parents had to sign this paper allowing me to stay on at sixth form, but Mum refused, saying it would be a waste of a good place and I would never amount to anything anyway. Thanks, Mum. All my hopes and dreams down the plughole. They're still inside me today.'

'So why don't you enrol now?'

'I don't have the confidence. This is what they've done to me. The only confidence I have is what Ian has given me. He tells me I could do it, but my mum's words have stuck, and I can't rid myself of them. I get that adrenalin, butterfly, panicky feeling whenever I think about following my dreams and going to college.'

'I went to college late, Laura, after Egypt . . .'

'You're stronger than me, Jacky. I could never have done what you did.'

We were silent for a moment. I wasn't sure she was right. We had both suffered in our own way. I'd been abused by my Egyptian husband, Laura by her family.

I straightened my stiff legs and continued. 'What was your first job?' I asked.

'At the dry cleaners. I worked there for four years, until I married Ian. I was actually offered the position of manageress, but I could see that it was a stressful job, so I didn't go for it. I spent a lot of my teenage years looking at other people and comparing myself to them. I would think, "If they can meet someone and get married, then so can I." I met Ian when he came into the dry cleaners, when I was seventeen. It was just magical. I looked up at him and my heart skipped a beat. He was my first and only boyfriend, and here we are twenty-three years later. He's wonderful. I don't know what I'd do without him, and I can't imagine how my life would have turned out if I hadn't met him.'

'How did your family react?'

'It was difficult for Ian. As a child I'd never been allowed to have friends, but now I was an adult earning my keep, so there wasn't a lot they could say. Jane did everything she could to split us up. She flirted madly with him, she tried kissing him, spreading rumours. We assume it must be down to the fact that she had no one and I did. It was obvious she was causing trouble, but none of the family intervened or told her to stop. It was a strange three years, but we knew we were going to be together. And he has stood by me, no matter what. We have been to hell and back, because of all the baggage that I took into the marriage. It wasn't just a bit of baggage, it was trunkloads of the stuff. It put us on the line once or twice, but we have managed to struggle through, seeking help to be where we are today.'

'And where is that?'

Lara smiled wryly. 'Believe it or not, I see us as a solid, wonderful family: Mum, Dad, Jack and Jess. My family is my world, and I wanted to put absolutely everything into my relationship with them. But because of what happened to me, I am still struggling to come to terms with the fact that it is okay to do this. I won't say that all these inhibitions have ruined my relationship with my son, Jack, but it has certainly suffered. When he reached the age of eight, all I could relate to was that boys and men hurt me. Jane, when all is said and done, effectively changed from a girl into a tomboy and began hurting me; my father did the same; my brothers were gradually turned against me. Even though I was an adult, all this overwhelmed me and resulted in me pushing him away. I love him to bits; he's my lad and I want the best for him. Yet I still pushed him away. It hurt him, I know that and I'm not proud of it. I can't move on, because the abuse has never stopped. Jack has become a casualty of my state of mind.'

'And Jess?'

'I haven't had such problems with Jess. Ian and I have supported her through school whenever she struggled and helped her build up her confidence. She is a quiet, contented and well-balanced young lady.'

'What about your state of mind now?'

'Okay. Here goes. I'm frightened of being alone, no, of loneliness. Fear of rejection holds me back all the time. I'm always concerned about what people think of me. In difficult situations, I tend to panic and look for someone to tell me what to do. When things go wrong, I automatically think, "What have *I* done wrong?" I cry when I'm angry. I'm continually altering my behaviour in order to gain the approval of my parents. I always feel like a naughty child in their presence. There is still a lonely little eight-year-old girl inside me, crying out for her mum and sister to love her again. I still long for my long-lost parents I knew and loved up to the age of eight, who would give me the childhood I've missed out on. This is why I wanted to give my children the best ever memories of their childhood. Sadly, with Jack, the barriers were just too great, but I try to support both of my children equally.'

'What sort of relationship do you have with your parents now?'

'We go round to their house to see them every Christmas. Everyone goes round for Christmas dinner and Christmas tea. Life plods on like most families. But every so often, things flare up again. I go round and clean for them, fetch bits of shopping, do what I can. Maybe this way there's a chance that one day they'll accept me, come to love me, or even just notice me. It's never appreciated, but I do it anyway. After all, they're my parents.'

Laura's amazing. She'll never know it, but she's dealt with her past in order that she can have a fulfilling relationship with her husband and two children. She hasn't turned her back on her parents, she doesn't interfere with the lives of her siblings and she isn't embittered or full of hatred as a result of her horrific experiences. Outwardly she's a happy, thoughtful, optimistic woman and a terrific friend. A heroine.

I put up with terrible physical abuse in my marriage. It's not the sort of thing you can compare, but to me what Laura had suffered was really much worse. It wasn't that my husband didn't love me. In his own way, I know that he did. But as a proud Moslem, he failed to provide me and our two daughters with the life he had envisaged. We relied on the generosity of his father and my work as an English teacher. That was so shameful to Omar that he took it out on me. Laura's abuse was not only physical, but psychological and very traumatic. She was an innocent child and the effects of that abuse have remained throughout adolescence and adulthood. For her there is no end; there can be no closure. In contrast, I always had a loving mum and dad at home in England on whose support and love I could rely, whatever I did. Laura's whole family shut her out and made her invisible. She had no choice.

12

Grace

Monday morning. I arose bright and early, eager to start another week. When the rest of the family had finally departed for work and school, I sat at my desk, preparing to trawl through the emails and other paperwork, before settling down to write. Half an hour later, yawning, I decided to read one more email and stop for a cup of tea.

I never got round to making the tea. I even forgot it was Monday morning. The next email was from a lady called Grace in Canada.

'Mum sent me your book, *Fatwa: Living with a Death Threat*. It was my birthday on Friday,' she wrote. 'I have loads of time on my hands and I read it in two days. Then I saw the website on the back cover. I mean, I don't know anything about you, but somehow that makes it okay. Pouring my heart out to a stranger. Safer somehow.

'Look at me,' she went on. 'I'm on automatic pilot. I thought all I ever wanted was a home and a family. Well, it is. I've worked so hard for so long, concentrating everything on them, to the exclusion of everything else. I should be happy, contented, fulfilled. Except that suddenly I find myself in a house I don't recognise. No longer "home", my children have left and my husband was never really there in the first place.'

As I read, I glanced around at my own home; bits of homework lying on the side, a muddy pair of football boots on the drainer, the cat sprawled out on the piano stool and the dog at my feet. I felt comfortable here; able to be me. How different my previous home in Egypt had been. I had felt like a stranger in it. And now, Grace was telling me the same thing about her home.

'Sounds like you spent so much time on your home and family, you forgot about you,' I replied. 'What do you like doing? Did you ever work? Do you have many friends?'

'My life is this house, my husband and the children. Twin boys and a girl don't leave much room for work or friends. I don't know who I am any more.'

I was flattered that she'd chosen me to offload onto. I replied instantly, my fingers flying over the keys. 'So if the children have left and your husband is out at work, how do you fill your days?'

'Housework. Cooking. Ironing. Daytime TV. I feel a bit like a volcano, ready to erupt. I had a bit of a do the other day.'

I was intrigued. I wanted to know more, but the email system was so fragmented. Frowning at the screen, I suddenly thought of MSN. We could communicate via instant messaging and chat properly online. As I wrote the idea down to email Grace, I knew it was the perfect solution. We could write our messages and they would send immediately. All our conversation would be on the screen to refer back to if we wanted. Waiting for the reply to this suggestion, I could feel my stomach churning with anticipation and excitement.

Grace seemed just as delighted at the idea. The whole set-up process took a mere twenty minutes. Now we could really get down to the nitty-gritty. I found myself wanting to know more about Grace's state of mind. Obviously, she was getting to the stage where ironing shirts just wasn't enough. I mulled over the last thing she'd mentioned, about to erupt. What had happened to cause that, I wondered.

I thought back to the days of my own first marriage to Omar in Egypt. It had been easier for me to accept my invisibility back then. Until my brutal husband laid his hands on my daughter, Leila, I had realised the futility of fighting back and accepted everything he chose to throw at me. For me, the catalyst had been his treatment of Leila.

'Okay then, Grace,' I wrote. 'This "bit of a do" you had. Can you describe it to me? Where you were, how you felt, what you were thinking?'

I watched my typewritten words flash into the instant messaging box. At the bottom of the screen, I was informed that Grace was typing a message.

Just a few seconds later, her reply appeared, 'I'll try.'

The next reply from Grace took her a long time to write. I knew she was typing the whole time, as my computer told me she was writing a message. Wanting to keep myself occupied, I whipped round the whole house with the vacuum, put on a load of washing and put out the rubbish, watching the screen intermittently. I finally settled down in front of the screen with a tuna sandwich and a glass of orange juice. When the message finally showed up, I realised she was indeed pouring out her heart to me. It had taken her forty minutes to write.

'It was Friday,' she started. 'My birthday. Brad had risen, showered and left for work without mentioning it, just the usual peck on the cheek. The postman brought parcels and a lovely card from Mum in England, but none from the children. I was doing the ironing, lost in thought, wondering if Brad was planning a surprise for later, when the shrill, relentless trill of the phone interrupted my reverie. I stood the iron carefully on its end before moving to answer. It was my daughter, Evie.

' "Mom? Hi, it's me. Happy birthday. Joe's taking us on the slopes for the whole day. Wish me luck. Maybe I'll come over next weekend. I'll bring your card then. Have a good one. Byeee." '

'Staring at the receiver,' Grace continued, 'I shivered impulsively. A huge log fire burned hungrily, spreading a warm glow throughout the kitchen, reaching out to every corner. But I felt cold. Worry, doubt, fear, tension suddenly swept over me in waves, enveloping and stifling me, until I couldn't breathe. I dropped the handset, yanked open the back door and stood shakily on the porch, turning my face skywards, letting the snowflakes caress me as they fell. The snowflake tears dripped down my cheeks and gradually melted away as the panic subsided.

'The grandfather clock sprang into life, shouting at me with every persistent chime, "Pull yourself together." Ten o'clock. Ten reminders. Enough for me to pull on my tough image like an old jumper and continue with the chores.'

I stared at the screen, eventually replying, 'Why have you stopped there?'

'That's all of it. My "bit of a do". I regained control. I'm okay now,' she replied.

I felt a rush of sympathy for her. 'Is that how you're dealing with it, then? Brushing your feelings under the carpet? Can't you have a word with Brad?'

Her reply came quickly. 'I tried that on Friday night. The panic attack scared me, so when Brad's secretary phoned to say he'd booked a table for us at Rinaldo's for seven-thirty, I decided to tackle him then. Usually he's so preoccupied with his work and avoids personal conversations. I made a special effort getting ready and we were relaxed together in the car on the way to the restaurant. "After the main course, I'll bring it up," I thought. Only when the time came, I was suddenly a bag of nerves. I escaped to the Ladies.

'Breathing deeply, I admired myself in the mirror. The dress had been an extravagance, there was no denying it. "Not bad for forty-eight," I whispered, smoothing the silky black material against my flat stomach. ' "Grace Saunders, you scrub up very well, although I say it myself." Smiling, I touched up my lipstick and walked elegantly towards the dinner table, aware of the attention from other diners.

' "I've ordered dessert for us both." Brad looked up, unsmiling in contrast. "What do you find to do in the washroom that takes so long?"

'I remember laughing, to ease his frustration. "Oh, come on, Brad. It takes time to look this good. Pour me a glass of wine, will you?"

'As I leaned across the table to take his hand, Tchaikovsky's *1812 Overture* invaded the room. Hurriedly, Brad answered his phone. My heart sank. Wine, food, wife were forgotten as he made plans to meet up with a colleague later that very evening. My golden opportunity was lost before my very eyes.'

'Didn't you ask him to postpone his meeting?' I asked.

'No point,' she answered. 'He'd just have resented me for asking, so we'd never have gotten round to any form of serious chat.'

'Did he at least give you a birthday present?'

She replied bitterly, 'Oh yes. Now, let's see, how did it go? In the car on the way home. His exact words were, "You know how it is, honey." Brad was apologetic in the car. He had been preoccupied since the phone call and only then remembered to reach into his pocket and hand me a blue box, with the words, "Happy birthday. I'll try not to be late." '

I could almost feel her pain. 'And was he?'

'Late? Of course. I'd had a dose of my mum by the time he got in, but before she called I was in bits.'

It was becoming obvious that Grace's mum was a firm source of emotional support and probably the only one. I wanted to know more. 'Tell me all about her call,' I said. 'Exactly what she said.'

'Well, the phone rang just before midnight. I was sitting up in bed, quietly crying. The conversation went something like:

' "Hello, Grace?"

' "Oh, hi, Mum. It's really good to hear your voice." I wiped my eyes dry as I spoke.

' "It's not too late over there, is it? Only I get so confused with the time difference, you being all the way over in Canada."

' "It's just right," I said, smiling in spite of myself. How long had it been? Nearly twenty-six years. Mum would never get the hang of it, just as she would never get used to her daughter leaving Manchester for Toronto.

' "Tell me all about your day then, pet. Did those grand-children of mine cook for you?"

' "Great day, Mum," I said, ironically. "Evie rang briefly, still besotted with Joe. They're snowboarding this weekend. No word from Jamie or Alex. Brad took me out for dinner, but had to go back to work. He gave me a pair of gold earrings. They're obviously expensive."

'I remember glancing in the mirror, tilting my head slightly until the large teardrop of gold in my right ear caught the light, hanging like an apology in the air. I could feel the panic rising again, but Mum's voice brought me back to the conversation.

' "Wait till I get my hands on those twins. They're getting beyond themselves," she fumed. "Too busy to visit their

mum on her birthday, now they're at university? Not even a
phone call? I'll give them too busy . . ."

' "Hang on, Mum, they probably won't have remembered," I started, and then stopped myself.

' "Why am I defending them?" I wondered.

' "Well, they should have," she replied angrily. "And that
husband of yours. You hardly ever see him. I wish I was
there. I'd give them all a piece of my mind, I would. I'd tell
them to get off their butts as they call them and go and find
you . . ."

'The tears returned as quickly as I'd wiped them away.
"But where would they go to find me?" I thought. "Where is
that woman they call 'Mum'? I can't even find myself any
more. I'm completely lost . . ." '

* * *

Gradually, Grace and I built up a strong relationship. We
set aside specific times to be online together. Although
morning for her meant teatime for me, it worked well. For
me, Grace started to become a major figure in my life. As
the layers and inhibitions fell away, we built up an unfathom-
able trust, enabling us to tell each other things, knowing
they would never go any further. I was happy to think I
might be of help to Grace, but equally I was enjoying the
benefits of such a close, genuine relationship.

'I've become invisible,' Grace complained. 'My children
don't know when my birthday is, my husband makes me feel
guilty for keeping him away from his colleagues. It never
occurs to any one of them that I might have feelings, for

God's sake. I've cooked, cleaned and waited on them for all these years . . .'

'Do you still love Brad?' I asked.

'Of course.'

Her reply didn't surprise me in the least. She would automatically say this, to justify her existence, almost as part of her household routine: do chores, chat with neighbour, go shopping, cook supper, love husband . . . I would have to try another tack.

'So how did you two meet?' I asked.

'We met at Oxford. I can see him now. Crumpled shirt, smudged glasses, hair that always stuck up on one side. Not your typical blonde Adonis. We were on opposing sides of the Debating Society one week, arguing for and against the class system in modern-day England. That was it. For both of us. True love. Forever. Wherever we decided to go from that point on, it would always be together.'

'And where was that?'

'Well, that's the other thing. I flew to the other side of the world with him, without a care in the world, as if I was just popping to the Spar shop. Where he went, I went. End of. I gave up everything I knew.'

'What did Brad give up, Grace?'

*   *   *

During the following month, we spoke almost daily. Grace painted a detailed but drab watercolour of her life, one I would certainly have passed by in an art gallery. Grace poured out her heart, while I listened, throwing in the odd question here and there, biding my time until I had the full picture.

It felt strange for me, being on the other side. Listening to someone else's problems, I mean. All these women were writing in to the website and I was trying to help. At the end of the day, I had no idea if it was a good or a bad thing. I was inexperienced and under-qualified to give advice, so what exactly did I think I was doing? All I knew was, if there had been someone out there for me when I felt alone, I would have jumped at the chance to talk to them. The point being, I couldn't talk to anyone around me. It would have been too dangerous. If I had confided in my friends or my parents that I was so unhappy that I regularly stood on the balcony of our tiny fourth-floor flat willing myself to jump off, someone would have said something. Two reasons prevented me from jumping. First, the children would be swallowed up by the family, married off at a young age and never know about me, England or its heritage. Second, I could never be absolutely sure I would die. Four floors up wasn't that high and I certainly wouldn't be able to cope in a rickety old wheelchair for the rest of my life. If I had had access to a computer and the opportunity to offload my fears onto a complete stranger, I would have taken it. I was completely lost, with no one to turn to. A stranger would have been the ideal solution.

Grace was indeed lost. Somehow she'd moulded herself into this plastic, efficient superwoman, always immaculate, concerned only with meeting the needs of Brad and the children, and running a smooth, orderly household. A tough job, it had been an adequate distraction from facing up to what she really wanted, and had completely taken over her life.

It's a known fact that if you tell someone something about themselves for long enough, eventually they'll believe it. So it was no surprise to me when Grace complained that the family took her for granted.

'In a way, you know, you can't really blame them,' I said. 'You've worked hard at being efficient, doing everything for them for years, making no demands whatsoever. So naturally, they have come to put themselves first too. At your expense. How would they feel if they let you down? "Oh, it doesn't matter. Mom won't mind. She'll understand." Because, you know why? They're right. You would. They don't feel your hurt, because you don't ever show it.'

There was no reply. I had never given an opinion up to this point. But now I had. I couldn't take it back. How would she react? What was she thinking? Grace didn't reply. But I knew that our relationship was strong enough now for me to begin pushing her into positive action. It would take a lot of guts on her behalf, but we both knew that this was why she had contacted me in the first place.

I continued gently. 'I think the time has come for you to face up to your feelings and show your family how you feel. You need to start making demands on their time, so that they see you in a new light. We'll talk later. Bye.'

The boundaries had changed. No longer able to remain the

passive listener, I knew my role as an anonymous, sympathetic ear and counsellor had come to an inevitable end.

Over the past three weeks, I had also shared intimate thoughts of my own with Grace. Like me, she had dutifully listened, always interested, always sympathetic. Never once had we offered strong opinions or criticised one another. Always supportive, never judgmental. Sighing, I resolutely pressed the send button and went to wake the dog. I could do with a good walk.

* * *

The cold air bit into my neck and round my ears; I wished I'd wrapped up warmer. I pulled up the collar of my jacket and pushed my hands deep into my pockets. The sky was very blue and clear. It would probably snow later, I thought, watching Henry bound up to the muddiest puddle at the edge of the field and roll over in it happily. Result? Wet, muddy dog. My reaction was initially one of frustration.

'Oh, Henry, do you have to?' I began, and then stopped myself. I picked up a stick and threw it as far as I could, watching Henry fleeing delightedly across the field in hot pursuit.

'Correction,' I muttered. 'Wet, muddy, *contented* dog. Blow the kitchen floor. Lighten up, my girl. Let Henry be Henry.'

I decided to do the same with Grace and give her time to respond without pestering her. It was two days before she contacted me, and not at our usual time. It must have been in the middle of the night for her. I had just unloaded the weekly shop from the boot of the car. Tesco carrier bags littered the whole of the kitchen floor and I was loading up the fridge, when the familiar sound of MSN jingled out from the computer. Leaving the fridge door wide open, I made my way to the computer and clicked on the link.

'I know what I want.'

This was Grace with a difference; I could sense it in those five short words. Something had changed.

Sitting down, I wrote, 'Glad you're still talking to me.' And then, 'Sorry about the other day . . .'

'You were right. I'm to blame,' she replied bluntly.

'No, I never said . . . I mean, I wasn't trying to . . .' I trailed off, lost for words.

'Brad's having an affair.'

A statement of fact, not blurted out with emotion, just bare words.

'The old cliché comes to Toronto,' she mocked. 'Brad and his blonde bimbo of a secretary. Except that she has short, red hair.'

'You've seen her?'

'Does it matter? She exists, that's what matters. This has been going on for the best part of a year and it never once crossed my mind to doubt his excuses. *That's* what matters. The irony of it. I was so trusting or blind that he didn't even make much effort to cover his tracks. There are entries in his diary with her name, time, everything. Once I opened my eyes, everything was there for me to see. I simply followed him.'

I was bowled over. 'Wow, Grace. Well done. When?'

'Thursday night. I drove to her place and sat outside.'

'And?' I was bursting for more information. This was big news.

'It was freezing,' continued Grace. 'I hardly felt the cold, just pulled my scarf tighter and tucked it firmly into the folds of my coat. I wasn't sure of the way and it was snowing hard. I drove slowly. All I could hear was the sound of the tyres crunching noisily over the snow.

'Eventually I came to the street. I chose the darkest place to park and switched off the engine. I sat very still. And I waited. The digital clock on the dashboard clicked as it registered 22:12. Sixty-three minutes later, my patience was rewarded. Brad's car drew up and stopped outside an apartment block. Instinctively, I shrank back, pressing myself against the soft leather of the seat, allowing myself only the tiniest shard of vision. It wasn't much, but enough to slice through my very being, as there, in front of my very eyes, my husband kissed and canoodled with another woman.'

The fridge began its relentless quest of alerting my attention, by bleeping loudly. I hardly noticed, as I typed in the words, 'So what are you going to do?'

The answer was swift and unexpected. 'Leave him, of course.'

* * *

It took Grace a mere three days to book a flight, make arrangements to stay with her mother and pack her life into two smart Louis Vuitton suitcases. She kept me informed every step of the way.

On the morning of her flight, she emailed me for the final time from her Toronto home. 'Hi, Jacky. The grandfather clock's just whirred into action to chime the hour. "Today's the day, today's the day," it's saying. Ten times. I've just finished the ironing.'

I was amazed. 'The what?'

'The ironing. Don't worry. I feel really calm. I've just hung the last shirt up in his wardrobe for him. Now Brad really will appreciate me.'

Over the next few days, I could only imagine what was happening to Grace. Whatever I was doing, she was always at the forefront of my mind. Did she actually leave? Where was she now? What happened with Brad? How was she coping? The questions revolved around my head constantly. It was agonising, not being able to contact her. I had trusted her with my phone number but, other than that, I had no way of contacting her at all. I would just have to wait.

A week later, the phone rang.

'Jacky? Grace here. How are you?'

She sounded excited. Her voice was deeper than I'd imagined. I almost cried with relief at finally hearing from her. Choking back the tears, I replied, 'It's great to hear your voice, Grace. I'm fine. More importantly, how are things with you?'

'Good. Mum's been great. Very emotional about having me back home again. She keeps hugging me and shedding a few tears. We talk a lot. It's funny. I've gotten so used to talking to the wall or the clock. It's strange to have someone there who is actually interested in what you have to say.'

'And Brad. What about him? Did you tell him you were leaving?' I asked. 'Tell me everything from the beginning,' I reminded her. 'Don't leave anything out.'

'Well, if it wasn't so tragic, it would be funny,' she replied. 'I left at eleven in the morning and Brad is usually home around seven. He actually came home and showered before realising I'd gone. It was the shirts that did it.'

I didn't understand. 'The shirts?'

She laughed, a deep, gravelly sound that echoed gently down the phone. 'Yes. He found them in the wardrobe.'

I was even more baffled than before. 'But isn't that where he'd expect to find them?'

'Listen, Jacky, I'll start over. When he'd finally gotten it into his brain that I had left, he phoned me here at Mum's. He was so uptight. Honestly, he totally freaked out, babbling on about what had happened when he'd got home, not giving me a chance to answer him or anything. Anyway, I'll give you the gist of what he said.'

She put on this dramatic, hushed voice and continued, 'The house was strangely silent; I was always there at the door to greet him, whatever the time of day. The fire in the kitchen had gone out, the familiar smell of home cooking now replaced by one of stale smoke. There was a chill in the air as he passed through the rooms, noting the newspapers strewn exactly where he'd left them, his dressing-gown draped over the banister. The unfamiliar, the unexpected created an unfriendly atmosphere, making him very uneasy. Apparently he called out my name several times, and that he'd just popped in to shower and change for another meeting.'

I giggled. 'This is so much better than emails. I can imagine myself right there in the house, watching him.'

'Listen. It gets better,' said Grace. 'Now we come to the good bit. Sweet revenge.' Her voice changed once more for the narration. 'Half an hour later, wrapped in only a towel, Brad stared in horror at the contents of his wardrobe. Every single item, every shirt, jacket, even the pants hanging neatly in place had one thing in common: a burnt hole on the front, the exact size and shape of the iron.'

I clamped my hand over my mouth as the realisation dawned. All that ironing. Every single shirt. Ruined. And I'd thought she was merely being her usual efficient self before she left, leaving everything in order.

'He must have been horrified. You really knew how to let him know you meant business, Grace. How clever of you,' I said with a giggle. 'What do you think he did then?'

Grace cleared her throat and continued, her husky voice transporting me into that very bedroom, as if I were there, watching Brad's reaction. 'He sat heavily on the bed, the realisation that I had gone suddenly smacking him hard in the face. Straight ahead of him, beside the window seat, he caught sight of the envelope, out of place on the usually bare coffee table.

'All other plans long forgotten, he moved quietly to where

the envelope lay and traced his name with his finger, written neatly in my small handwriting. Everything that he dreaded was contained within such a slim, white envelope. This was his final thought as fear swooped uninvited from the envelope to envelop him instead.

'Dusk fell as he sat at the window and read. And as he read, he began to understand that his life as he knew it would never be the same. As the sentences reached his mind, he could see me sitting calmly on the window seat beside him, making him listen, making him see what he refused to see, making him confront where they were, making him see things from my point of view.'

Grace threw back her head and laughed heartily on the phone. 'How was that? Mr Brad Saunders. Forty-eight, fit for his age, self-assured, successful, in control of his life. Until that day. I bet he wishes he had never come home. That he had never opened that letter.'

'Brilliant.' How Grace had changed. 'What did the letter say?'

'In a minute,' she replied. 'I also made him do something he's not done for years and years. I know, because he did it again on the phone when he called.'

'What did he do?'

'He cried.'

For a moment I felt sorry for Brad. But this was only fleeting, as Grace went on immediately. 'Now imagine him reading the letter,' she said, clearing her throat. 'This is what it said:

'My Darling Brad,

All my life I have loved you and we once swore to be together forever. Forever ended today.

You chose someone else, but I let it happen. I let you put me second. So Little Miss Redhead got the first prize.

I've made an important decision. I don't want to be second any more. I want to be first.

I'm returning to England to be away from the kids and away from you, where I have only me to consider. Twenty-six years ago I left my own mum, and it's taken all this time for me to appreciate how she felt, when mine fled the nest without a care. Believe me, it hurts. I never gave her a second thought, just like Evie, Jamie and Alex. Mums have a way of covering up such feelings. Well, I'm going to make sure I make it up to mine now.

This is my time to rediscover me. I still love you, but somehow we lost each other along the way. I did everything you ever wanted, yet I never asked you for a thing. Is that why you got so used to giving me nothing?

Goodbye Brad. Be happy,

Grace.'

She was silent.

I was impressed. 'Grace, you certainly know how to hit a man where it hurts,' I said. 'No reproaches, no accusations. Brilliant.' My mind suddenly took me back to the bedroom with Brad and the letter. 'So when he had finished crying . . .'

'. . . he called me up here. Oh, Jacky, he was so down, crying, begging me to come back and start over.'

That didn't surprise me. 'How did that make you feel?' I asked.

'Well, I was sort of expecting it,' she replied. 'But it was still a shock to hear him actually saying the words. And do you know what else? We had our first conversation in years. You know, where one person speaks, the other listens and then responds? After he had babbled on, going through every single thing he'd done up to finding the letter, he finally burst into tears, sobbing openly. Then he blew his nose, apologised and went sort of quiet.'

'Quiet? What do you mean?'

'Brad doesn't do quiet,' Grace explained wryly. 'He fills every silence with what he has to say and either hangs up or leaves. No, this time, he quietened down and began to ask me questions. At first, I gave insignificant, airy answers, not expecting him to take any notice of what I said. But he pressed for more, hanging on my every word. It was seriously weird. I mean, he usually waits for me to finish and then says what's on his mind, as if I'm in the way with my words. He really listened to me this time, Jacky.'

I took a deep breath and asked the $64,000 question. 'Did he tempt you into considering going back?' I asked, crossing my fingers as I did so.

I needn't have bothered.

'Oh, no.' Grace's tone was determined. 'But he's certainly more attractive from the other side of the world.'

Grace and I began phoning one another weekly, on a Tuesday evening after tea. Brad didn't give up; on the contrary, he bombarded Grace with calls, flowers, even letters. Three weeks after her arrival, she phoned with some news.

'He's sent me a poem. Jacky, this is a different Brad.'

'What sort of poem?'

Grace sounded excited. 'Well, the original's by Leonard Cohen and about a girl called Annie, but he's replaced "Annie" with "Grace".'

'So? Anyone can do that. You must admit, it's a bit cheesy, Grace.'

'I don't think so. We read quite a bit of poetry in our student days, but never since. I left all my books behind in England. We both liked Cohen's work. No, Jacky. This says to me that he's making a real effort.'

'So what's the poem?'

'I'll read it as Cohen wrote it,' replied Grace.

With Annie gone
Whose eyes to compare
With the morning sun?
Not that I did compare.
But I do compare
Now that she's gone.

'What do you think?' she asked eagerly.

'I think it's sad that he only noticed you when you'd gone or listened to you when you weren't there. I think he's blown it big time. And I think he knows it,' I replied drily. I was determined not to pull any punches at this stage.

'He's really dumped Little Miss Redhead, he's not just saying it. He wants me back,' she continued, ignoring my comments.

I sighed. 'Well, of course he does. That's obvious. Little Miss Redhead won't be able to iron his shirts the way you did.'

Grace laughed. 'You can say that again.'

Not only Brad, but also Evie, Jamie and Alex bombarded Grace continually with emails and phone calls. Whereas the children were horrified that their mother could even think of doing such a thing, and accused her of being selfish and thoughtless, ending predictably with, 'What about them?', Brad took a different approach.

In short, he was devastated and took it upon himself to try and understand what was going on in Grace's mind. He tried to woo her, all over again.

'He wants to come over to England to see me,' Grace told me, a week later. 'For a fortnight. Says he'll take leave. Leave! For God's sake, Jacky, he never does that. Shall I say, "Yes"?'

'Do you want to say, "Yes"?'

'Yes, yes, yes!' Grace replied.

'There's your answer, then. You'd better get on the phone. Good luck.'

It was hard for me, being so involved in Grace's life, to step back for a fortnight and let her get on with it. Her life had somehow become entwined with my own; I had set aside time for her that was special and I missed her. So I felt an extra thrill when she contacted me the day after Brad's return to Toronto.

'Hi, Jacky. Wonderful time had by all. He even charmed the pants off Mum. I know he was bound to make an effort, but get this. He knows we can't go back to where we were. So he's made me an offer. He says, last time I gave up everything to follow him. So this time, he's prepared to give up everything to follow me. Can you believe it?'

I was baffled. 'Believe it? I don't understand it. Where would you live? What would you live on? What about the kids?'

'I told him my future was in England. I want to follow up my degree in English literature and see if I can get some lecturing work. Did I mention I got a first? Anyway, this didn't faze Brad at all. He just wants us to be together again. He keeps saying his job means nothing without me.'

'Just a few years late in coming,' I replied. 'And the kids?'

'Well, I haven't agreed to anything yet. I'm determined to take things slowly – at my pace. Brad will have to wait for me. And if we do decide to give this a try, then the kids'll have two choices: like it or lump it.'

'My goodness, how you've changed.'

'No, I've just made myself visible again.'

* * *

The following month, Brad suggested they take a holiday together and, this time, I was happy for Grace. Maybe they did have a future together.

'Oh, Jacky, it's the holiday of a lifetime. Three weeks in Thailand, taking in Christmas and New Year, ending with three days in Bangkok. I'll make my decision then. Well, actually, I've already decided, but I'll make him sweat a bit. It'll be a second honeymoon. I really do love him, you know.'

I smiled as I said, 'I know you do. And you know what? This time you'll both be happy for the rest of your lives.'

At the moment, I'm sitting at home staring at a few lines of a poem, brought to my attention by a very special person. It goes like this:

With Annie gone,
Whose eyes to compare
With the morning sun?
Not that I did compare.
But I do compare
Now that she's gone.

Leonard Cohen must have felt the pain of loss to come up with such a poignant combination of words. They certainly mean a hell of a lot to me.

Grace and Brad flew off to Thailand the week before Christmas, intent on making a fresh start and looking forward, not back. I was content to think about the wonderful time they were having and wait for a postcard.

No one could have predicted the terrible natural disaster that descended upon the Asian coastline, or the force with which it devastated whole villages and settlements.

The all-powerful tsunami invaded and conquered Asia on the morning of Boxing Day, 2004. The massive tidal wave wiped out complete communities and a whole generation of children.

Tourists from all over the world were also victims, swept away, drowned or killed by debris as it smashed into them in the water.

In England, on Sky television, lists of survivors were put on screen and there were websites on which to look for people. Of Grace and Brad, there was no news. Nothing. Grace's mother is frantic with worry, and it has fallen on her unfortunate shoulders to fly out and search for her daughter. A task no mother should ever have to undergo.

It is now the first week of February. Still no news. Grace's mother has returned, desolate, broken, lost. Although our hearts are screaming for us to believe that they will be found alive and well, as time goes on, hope fades and the belief that they have perished becomes more real.

The postman delivered a postcard yesterday. From a place called Cha-Am, in Thailand. It featured Marukkhathaiwain Palace, a construction on stilts on the beach, yellow with a red roof. I wonder if it's still there? The postcard was from Grace. It was a happy postcard, telling me how wonderful the country was, how cheap things were and how fantastic the fresh fish tasted. Ironically, the last words she wrote were, 'Take care.'

13

Yasmine

I turned over, sticking my leg on the top of the sheet and burying my head in the pillow, willing sleep to descend upon me. It was a sweltering night, hot and sticky with no breeze. My hair clung to my cheeks in damp clumps and my head ached naggingly. I tried to ignore everything and concentrate on getting to sleep, but it was no use. I was wide awake.

Wearily I squinted up to the ceiling where the large red figures reflected eerily: 01:54.

'Great Christmas present. The clock of the future,' I mused, remembering the day I had ripped off the wrapping and sworn I'd never get used to a reflecting clock; I was quite happy with the cracked bedside one, thank you. My husband Ben had quietly installed this newfangled invention, and now I merely had to lie back and stare up to locate the time. Marvellous.

I swung both legs over the side of the bed and tiptoed downstairs to the kitchen to make a cup of tea. It was a peaceful, still night. I stared out of the window into the blackness, the silence disturbed only by the humming of the kettle.

'You have mail, madam.'

The voice boomed out from the computer screen. Startled, I crossed over to the desk and clicked on the butler notifier. Who on earth would be sending me mail at this hour?

The message was from an unknown sender and contained three simple words: 'Is it safe?'

Ambiguous to say the least. My curiosity, however, drove me to reply: 'Yes.'

I made the tea, sat at the desk and waited.

Five minutes ticked slowly by.

Then, 'Are you alone?'

I decided to reassure whoever it was, to let them get to the point. I replied, 'No one is in the room with me. Only my husband and son are here and they are sleeping. It is completely safe to continue.' A chill ran through me on that hot night, an intuition that something terrible was going to happen.

The person replied immediately. 'Thank you. But please confirm that you are Jacky Trevane.'

'This is Jacky.'

'Okay. Sorry. I'm very scared that someone will find out what I'm doing. I have to be so careful. My father is sleeping upstairs. If he awakes, I will have to stop talking to you.'

'That's fine. How can I help?'

'My name is Yasmine. I live with my parents, two brothers, a sister, my auntie and her daughter in Leicester. My uncle died last year and my auntie came to live with us. We are from Jordan, at least my parents are. I was born in England.

We are Moslems. I've just finished your book, *Fatwa*, and saw your website on the back cover. It made me think. Maybe you know someone I can turn to for help. I'm frightened for my life.'

I sat up and stared at the screen. Her words were tumbling out as if she was in a hurry, trying to tell me she was in trouble. If she was asking me, a complete stranger, then she must be afraid of the people around her. But whatever problem she was facing, what could I possibly do to help?

Wearily I pushed my hair out of my face and drank the last of the now tepid tea. I shouldn't get involved. Where would it lead? Even as these thoughts entered my mind, I knew I wouldn't heed them. I was hooked. 'Here goes then,' I muttered.

'How old are you, Yasmine?'

'Nineteen,' came the reply.

'Why are you in danger?'

'I had a cousin, Soha, who went to the same college as me. She loved styling her hair and experimenting with make-up, although her father would never approve of her wearing it outside the house. We would spend many evenings in my bedroom, gossiping and painting our nails. She was actually very good at it – you know, putting little diamonds and patterns on the nails, even the toes. Anyway, she began to resent having to cover her head whenever she attended college, and sometimes would be brave enough to remove it during the lunch-hour. She read *Cosmopolitan* magazine behind her father's back and smoked in the toilets. She was a happy, intelligent and spirited girl with an infectious optimism that was hard to ignore. She was usually surrounded by friends. Boys were attracted to her and she knew it. But she handled them so well, never getting close to anyone in particular or spending time alone with them. You know we can't . . .'

The correspondence suddenly came to an end. I supposed she had been interrupted. I sat there for half an hour. Nothing. Damn. What if she had got herself into more trouble by talking to me? What should I do?

I eventually decided to try and contact her. If she replied, fine. If she didn't, then I hadn't lost anything.

I wrote, 'Yasmine. Are you there?'

The reply was swift. 'Yes. I was crying . . . Too upset.'

I gave a sigh of relief. 'This is nerve-wracking, Yasmine. I would much rather talk to you. Do you have a mobile phone? Then we could chat freely when your parents aren't likely to overhear.'

I awoke late the next morning in a fluster, drove Adam to the school bus in my dressing-gown and returned to three strong cups of black coffee before showering and dressing. It had been 4.20 a.m. when I'd finally climbed into bed. Two and a half hours' sleep. I wandered into the bedroom to make the bed and slipped my hand inside the bottom pillowcase. My fingers closed around the piece of paper nestling there. I stared at Yasmine's number and the time, 12.30. I mustn't forget to call.

'Hi, Yasmine. It's Jacky. How are you today?'

'Hi, Jacky. Better, thanks. I'm at college, so we can talk freely.' She spoke quickly, adding a feeling of urgency to her soft voice.

'You were talking about your cousin,' I prompted her.

'Yes, Soha,' she replied. She took a deep breath. 'At sixteen she was brave, headstrong and daring. She worked hard and did well in her exams. The family was proud of her. In her final year, we were having lunch one day and a boy slipped a note into her bag, asking her to meet him alone later. Soha had no idea he had put it there. At home, she put her bag in the front room and went to help prepare supper. And that was it.'

I could hear a sob as Yasmine began to cry.

'Yasmine? What happened?'

She continued between huge sobs. 'Her father emptied out her bag and found the note. He was furious and wouldn't believe Soha's pleas of innocence. When he searched her room and found a lipstick in her coat pocket, he went mad, accusing her of bringing shame on the family and beating her around the face and head with a stick until she passed out. He locked her in her room, but she escaped through the window and came to our house. She threw stones up to my room and I let her in secretly through the back door. No one in my family would have let her in and I knew I'd be in trouble if they found out what I'd done, but I could see she was terrified. In our culture, you never get involved when a father is disciplining his family; he and his actions must be respected at all times and never questioned. We slept together in my bed that night, our arms wrapped tightly round each other.'

She paused. I was impatient. 'So what happened when she went back the next morning?' I asked. 'Did you go with her?'

'Back?' Yasmine's voice was reduced to a whimper. 'She didn't go back. We both knew she could never return to her family. Ever.'

I didn't understand. 'But surely her father would eventually calm down. Every family has their arguments and loses their temper,' I said.

'This was different,' replied Yasmine. 'Soha had been accused of bringing the family honour into question. This was no ordinary argument. She had no redress. The judgment was made and her fate sealed.'

'What do you mean, "Her fate was sealed?" '

'Bringing shame on a family is the most severe crime a girl can commit. It is punishable by death.'

'You mean . . .'

'Yes, Jacky, she could not go back. She would be returning to her death.'

Even though I understood the words, I couldn't comprehend what Yasmine was telling me. I said as much. 'That may be how things are in Jordan,' I replied, 'but we're in England. British law forbids such barbaric behaviour. It just would not happen here.'

Yasmine uttered a wry laugh. 'Jacky, for all that you have gone through, you are still so very naïve. Do you think for a moment that my father is bothered about laws? Compared to retaining the family honour, they are nothing to him. He is passionate about maintaining a shameless reputation. Yes, it certainly would happen here in England. It does happen.'

I was stunned. 'So what did you do?'

'Well, we planned Soha's escape. I was shaking with fear, as if we were discovered, I too would be punished. We phoned an English friend and Soha slipped out the next day and stayed there for a couple of nights. By then her father and brothers knew she had gone and had come to our house looking for her. They asked me loads of questions but I gave nothing away. That night she sent me a text saying she was leaving to go and live in London; that she loved me and would never forget me . . .'

'Oh, I'm so glad she got away. Does she still keep in touch?'

'She said it would be too dangerous. That was the last I heard of her, until . . .'

Yasmine fell silent.

'Until?' The suspense was killing me.

In a flat, emotionless, low voice, Yasmine continued. 'Six months went by with no news of Soha. Then, out of the blue, I received a frantic text message saying, "They've found me. Dear God, Yasmine, please help." Immediately I rang her number to speak to her, but it went straight to the answerphone. I was too late. I never spoke to her again.'

'Do you know where she is?'

'They murdered her,' Yasmine replied, her voice little more

than a whisper. 'Her father and brothers eventually tracked her down, forced their way into her flat and murdered her. They stabbed her through the heart and cut her throat so fiercely her head was half-severed. Her body was then disposed of. They returned to Leicester and told everyone that they had found a suitor for her in Jordan and that she had travelled that day for the impending marriage. All the family had to travel to Jordan for two weeks, so it appeared they had attended Soha's wedding. But there was no suitor and there was no wedding because my Soha is dead.'

I was in a daze. 'How can you be sure? At the end of the day, she was their daughter, their flesh and blood. They couldn't actually murder one of their own. Could they?'

'That was the whole point. Soha was no longer one of their own. She had brought shame on the family name and had to be cast out. Living in westernised society here in England, these views must seem a bit over the top, and I suppose that was one of Soha's mistakes. She didn't fully appreciate the implications of her wearing lipstick in public, or innocently chatting with boys. Excuse me.'

Yasmine paused to blow her nose. 'I know the murder took place, because her poor, distraught 13-year-old sister had overheard the family discussing the gory details. She had been paralysed with fear and I was the only person she could talk to. She chose me. Thank God, no one suspects she knows. The rest of her family go about their daily lives as if nothing has changed, their eyes cold and expressionless. I can't talk any more about it. I can't bear to think of it. We need to talk again to discuss my problem, Jacky. Is that okay with you?'

At home, I scoured the Internet for more information on honour killings. I was horrified to find that this barbaric behaviour is virtually commonplace in Moslem countries. In Pakistan, for example, women live in fear. Male relatives control them totally and many are murdered if they are merely suspected of bringing shame on the family. They can be shot, stabbed or even set on fire and burnt to death. Every year, not just one or two but hundreds of women are known to die as a result of honour killings. Most go unreported and almost all go unpunished.

I had assumed that this practice was in some way related to Islam, as it is Moslems who murder their womenfolk under this fragile premise. Yet as I read further reports, it became clear that killing for honour actually went against the teachings of Islam and there was no justification for it. Tradition triumphs over the true meaning of the Qu'ran and is so strong that it can turn the teachings of the Qu'ran into a licence to kill.

Fascinated, I widened my search to see if honour killings were ever performed on males for shameful behaviour. I found nothing. 'The gender issue raises its head once again,' I thought. 'Boys are allowed, expected even, to be boisterous, wild, disrespectful and adventurous on their journey to manhood. A freedom they all take for granted. In a sense they are incapable of bringing shame on the family, which makes shame a female crime.'

What was even more distressing was that this custom thrived in England, too. I discovered that twelve such murders had taken place in the last six months in the UK – and those were the ones the authorities were aware of. Was this just the tip of the iceberg? The accused were serving life sentences in our prisons, but there must be many more murderers walking freely on our streets, as in Soha's case. What were the real figures, I wondered. It made me shudder to think about it.

In Jordan, if any sentence is given at all, it is rarely more than six months. In Pakistan, Yemen, Afghanistan and many other countries, there is no legal framework to protect women from honour killings. Even the words distressed me. Honour killings! One word would suffice: murder, plain and simple.

A week later, I called Yasmine at our appointed time. She sounded brighter, almost pleased to speak to me, as if I had been accepted as her new-found confidante.

'Jacky, thank you for calling. I really need to explain my problem to you. Time is running out.'

I prayed that I would be able to offer some sort of help, however small, to alleviate this poor girl's plight.

'I'll do whatever I can, Yasmine,' I said.

'Basically, I've lived all my life in England. I have English friends and I'm happy here. Of course I can't speak to boys freely or go out on dates, but I'm okay with that. My best friend was always Soha. Now that she's gone, there's a gaping hole in my life and I can't seem to find as many reasons to smile any more. I had my nineteenth birthday last month and my parents sat me down and told me that it was time for me to marry. It was the last thing I was expecting to hear them say. They had encouraged me to work hard in school, get my GCSE's and go on to college. I'd sort of taken it for granted that I'd qualify as a beauty therapist and find a job in Leicester. Marriage, kids, the whole settling-down thing hadn't entered my head.'

'You must have thought about boyfriends, though. Doesn't every teenager?'

'Believe me Jacky, I was fine about it. The freedom of college gave me a sense of normality that other young English people had. I put off thinking about settling down until I'd sorted out a decent career first. Anyway, my father brought three eligible Jordanian men to the house to meet me, all of them cousins.'

'Cousins? That's a bit close, isn't it? Why did he want you to marry someone from your own family?'

'It's normal in our culture, even preferred,' replied Yasmine. 'I had no intention of getting married yet, so I rejected all three of them outright. My father seemed okay when I said, "No", but I now recognise his quiet response to be controlled anger. A week later, he told me he had betrothed me to a respectable Jordanian who lived in Jordan. Everything, even the dowry, had been discussed and agreed and all in my absence. This man is thirty-two years old and is losing his hair. How do they expect me to fly over and live happily ever after with a man I have never met? He is a

131

"good catch", according to mother, with his own house and business. I wanted to scream and shout that they had no right, that I would not marry this man. But somehow, after Soha, I lost my nerve. Everyone around me is rushing around in a frenzy, preparing for my big day. You've got to help me, Jacky. Please?'

'When are you due to fly out there?' I asked.

'Next month. The ninth.'

I looked at the calendar. It was the seventeenth. 'My God, that's only three weeks away.' I started to panic. 'Look, Yasmine, let's think sensibly about this. If you go, everyone in your family is happy but you. If you don't go, then what does that mean? Your family will never give in. So you will have to run away, just like Soha. Is that the life you want for yourself? Always on the run, never seeing or speaking to your family or any of your friends again?'

'No, of course I don't want that,' she replied quietly.

I was pacing up and down the dining-room, thinking on my feet. 'Either way, your life as you know it is over. You do realise that, don't you?'

'I suppose you're right, Jacky. I'm frightened.'

'And so you should be. The way I see it, you *do* have a choice. You go to Jordan and begin a new life as the Moslem wife of a Jordanian. You maintain the family honour. Everyone approves. Or, you make plans to leave Leicester and run away to start a different life as a different person. The trouble with this is that, like Soha, you will have brought the family into disrepute and they will hunt you down. You will be alone and frightened and have no one to talk to. This is definitely the dangerous option. And let's face it, Yasmine, you were forced into making these choices. You don't really want to run away. After what happened to Soha, can you honestly say that you're strong enough to go it alone? Once you decide, there's no going back. You have to be sure.'

'That's why I'm frightened,' said Yasmine. 'I don't want to go to Jordan and I don't want to run away.'

I could hear the desperation in her voice, laced with sadness. 'Yasmine, there are no other choices. You need to spend time alone to consider which road to choose. Call me whenever you want. But make your choice and stick to it.'

I couldn't sleep that night, despite the cool breeze. Yasmine's dilemma swam round and round in my mind. What would she decide? What would I do in her position? Now, at the grand old age of forty-something, I would choose the safer option and fly off into the sunset to be married. But would I have done that at the age of nineteen? Probably not. Definitely not. At twenty-three, I'd followed my heart and jumped into a different life, from which I'd had to escape. I've been hiding from that life for sixteen years now. In the morning, I'd start looking into ways that Yasmine could 'disappear', if she chose to.

Two days later, I was negotiating my shopping trolley between the crowded aisles in Tesco when my phone bleeped to let me know there was a message. A short message of three terrifying words, 'I have chosen.'

I left the trolley in the middle of the frozen food section

and hurried out to reply in peace. It was pouring with rain, so I sat in the car. 'Is it safe to call?' I typed in hurriedly, drumming my fingers on the dashboard waiting for her reply.

It came straight back. 'No. I'm going ahead with the marriage. It's for the best. I'll call you later.'

I couldn't help it. I sat in the car with tears pouring down my cheeks, watching the rain splatter onto the windscreen. My shoulders heaved and I sobbed. I cried for Soha, for Yasmine's bravery and for the bleak future that must surely be ahead of her. It would have been brave to run away. But far, far braver of Yasmine to walk away from everything that she knows to a future she already fears and resents. I prayed it would prove to be the right decision.

The next day, Yasmine called. 'Jacky, thank you. You have made me face what had to be faced. I am not so stupid that I can sit back and not heed what happened to Soha. If I chose that road, then I could expect no less. No, it has to be. I will be married next month and have babies.'

'You don't have to have children. One thing at a time,' I replied, trying desperately to lighten the tone of the conversation.

'It is a necessary requirement of marriage that a woman bears children,' said Yasmine solemnly.

I laughed. 'Says who? You sound as if you're quoting from some sort of manual.'

'I wasn't joking, Jacky. It's an integral part of our culture. So much so, that if I had problems conceiving it would be sufficient grounds for my husband to divorce me and cast me out. Oh, and it's infinitely preferable to have sons. They are needed to support their elders when they grow up. So if I have only daughters, I will have to keep giving birth until I have a son. Women have no value. None at all.'

'How do you know this, all of a sudden?' I asked.

'My mother's teaching me how to behave and what to expect. We're not allowed to just go out when we want to. We have to be chaperoned. We have to have everything approved before we buy it, to be sure it's appropriate. And we can't drive. Can you believe it? It's entirely up to my husband's family and they don't think it's right.'

I remembered my ex-husband's family in Cairo and the power they had over me. I had been raped by Omar's brother, with no recriminations or blame. Even so, I believed Yasmine had reached the right decision.

'I think you've made a wise choice, Yasmine.'

She was silent.

*   *   *

It was Wednesday evening, ten days after our conversation. I was alone in the kitchen preparing tea, Adam was in his room blasting the house out with his drum practice and Ben was taking a shower. He came into the kitchen dressed only in a towel, switched on the telly, turned up the volume and sat at the breakfast bar.

'Sorry, love,' he shouted. 'This is the only place I can hear the television when Adam's on the drums. I want to watch the weather forecast.'

It was, therefore, amid an atmosphere of complete chaos,

television versus drums versus boiling kettle versus bubbling pans on the hob, that the newscaster announced the death of a 19-year-old Jordanian girl in Leicester.

The distressed truck driver had issued this statement: 'There was a group of girls standing at the side of the street, outside Miss Selfridge. I wasn't driving very fast. They approached the road as if waiting to cross. It happened so quickly. One minute she was standing with her mates, the next she was lying under the front of my truck. There was nothing I could have done. The ambulance was at the scene within five minutes, but she was pronounced dead on arrival at hospital. All she managed to say was, "I'm sorry" to the paramedic before passing away. A tragedy. Such a little thing. Had her whole life ahead of her.'

If only he knew.

In the end, Yasmine had taken control. In the face of two choices, where either one seemed intolerable, she had found a third. She had listened to what her parents wanted, she had seen Soha's fate and she had listened to me. Whatever she decided, she would lose her identity and the real Yasmine would eventually become invisible.

So she turned her back on these options. She remained true to herself.

And she made her choice.

14

Charlotte

The bell sounded for the end of the lesson and there was the usual shuffling of chairs and mounting volume of chatter as I dismissed the class, requesting that they handed in their books as they left. Quickly, I scanned the classroom, mentally checking that chairs had been left in place and no one had left anything behind. This was a challenging group: Year Eleven, Set Three French. Twenty-two testosterone-filled teenagers, notorious for getting away with murder if they could. I intended to make sure that this philosophy did not extend to my lessons. This required constant monitoring, particularly at the beginning and end of lessons. The sunlight blocked off the whole of the far corner so that I had to squint and shade my eyes with my hand to see properly.

It was then that I noticed.

'Billy, pick that up please. Your back is in far better condition than mine,' I barked. According to staff-room chitchat, throwing books was one of Billy's specialities. Not in my classroom. As Billy retrieved his book and handed it to me, I spoke through the sunlight to the back of the room,

'Stay behind for a minute, please, Charlotte. I need a

hand with these books if you don't mind.' I smiled at the group of girls at the back of the room, as Charlotte nodded in reply.

'Is there anything troubling you?' I asked.

We were alone in the classroom, away from other ears. Charlotte stared at the floor and shook her head. The light bore down on her wavy, auburn ponytail, giving it a multicoloured richness all the way down her back to her waist.

I tried again. 'They'll never know you've told me. As far as they know, you're helping me carry books.'

I reached over and gently tilted her face towards me, encouraging her to look at me, but her eyes remained downcast.

'There's nothing to tell,' she said finally, staring at her hands and picking at her fingers. I could see the skin around several of her fingers was sore, red and bitten away.

'I saw,' I continued.

That was enough for Charlotte to leave her fingers alone and look up at me, a scared, questioning look in her eyes.

'Not a lot gets past me, you know,' I said with a smile, trying to lighten the mood. 'I saw Jade hold your arm behind your back, while Danielle took your phone out of your pocket. Sharon tried to shield her, but I moved because of the sun and saw it all. Even the piece of paper she shoved at you.'

Silence. I gave it my last shot. 'Look, Charlotte. It seems to me that, if it was nothing, then you'd be happy to tell me all about it. The very fact that you're so secretive tells me that something's wrong. Now am I right, or am I right?' I gazed at her, half-smiling.

'You're right,' said Charlotte. 'They pretend to be my friends, but really they're just playing with me. They dared me to text this lad asking him out, but I wouldn't . . .'

'So they did it for you from your phone?' I asked.

Charlotte nodded miserably.

'Sneaky,' I said. 'And the note?'

She held out a crumpled piece of paper, torn from an exercise book. I frowned. I hadn't noticed that. Slowly, I read out the word, scrawled in large uneven capitals, 'CHICKEN'.

Tears splashed onto my desk as Charlotte began to cry.

'No, Charlotte. Here, dry your eyes. Quickly,' I ordered, handing her a tissue. 'That's the worst thing you can do,' I added. 'If I'm going to help you, then this conversation never took place. Do you understand?'

Laying both hands firmly on her trembling shoulders, I looked her straight in the eye. 'Jade, Danielle and Sharon could guess we've been talking if they see you all upset. That will mean only one thing. More trouble. Now pull yourself together and go to your next class. Take this note,' I added, scribbling a note to Mrs Harris explaining Charlotte's lateness.

'What will you do?' Charlotte asked, taking the note.

'Ask them about the note they wrote to you.'

Her eyes widened. 'You can't do that.'

'Why not?' I smiled. 'You dropped it when you picked up

this pile of books for me. Didn't you notice?'

To me, teaching's never just been about 'imparting knowledge'. The knowledge and understanding is only one part of it. And if the other parts aren't working properly, then that bit fails as well.

Teenagers are a tricky species. But if we, as teachers, treat them all the same, then we're doing a pretty poor job. We have a duty to try and understand them, in order to teach them. Toerags and nerds alike, they all have their anxieties, which almost always invade and threaten to annihilate the detailed lesson plans of us, the vulnerable teachers. We have a tough time setting standards, and an even tougher one maintaining them. But one of the most valuable and rewarding abilities we can have is to listen.

So that's what I try to do. I muddle along, taking a 'professional interest' in the students, but also confronting problems that arise, rather than leaving it to the next teacher or head of year to deal with. I've earned a fair amount of respect from the students, which I give back. I confronted the culprits about the note written to Charlotte and sent them off with a flea in their ear. They assured me that this would not happen again and I reminded them that there would be serious repercussions if there was any more trouble.

And that was it. No one reported anything further to me. I didn't notice any more inappropriate behaviour from Jade and her friends. Charlotte remained quiet during lessons, but then she always had been. She continued to tag along behind Jade and the others, always slightly on the outside of their tightly knit group. She didn't stay behind after lessons, or try to talk to me.

Outwardly, there was nothing happening to suggest that anything was wrong.

At the end of that academic year, I gave up teaching to concentrate on writing. My first book was doing well, and the website was well frequented.

Charlotte actually wrote to me via the website, a few weeks into the new term. She'd finished her GCSEs and left the school to study A levels at college.

'I wasn't sure how you'd feel if I wrote to you like this. But I couldn't speak to you at school. I just couldn't. They would have found out. Somehow. And then they would have made my life even more of a misery.'

I stared at her words. This was a cry for help. As if she had no one else to confide in. She needed a sympathetic ear. Should I get involved?

Eventually I decided to reply, although not straightaway. I left it for a day, and then kept things as light as possible.

'Hi, Charlotte. Nice to hear from you. Bet you're pleased with your French grade. Well done. At least you can put all the troubles at school behind you now and move on. How's college?'

She replied that afternoon.

'College is okay,' she wrote. 'There's this boy I like who keeps smiling at me. And I've started hanging around with a group of girls who catch the same bus.'

I was relieved. She had never really made a proper friend

at school, so this sounded very promising. Things were fine after all. I put Charlotte to the back of my mind and got on with the day.

The next morning there was another email from Charlotte in my Inbox.

'Sorry, Mrs Trevane, but I've read your book twice now and it's great. I really need someone to talk to and I know you'd understand. Would it be all right if I asked you things? I daredn't when I was at school, but this way it's different. Private. But I don't want to bother you if it's too much trouble or anything.'

Somehow I'd known there was something not quite right. And I admired her for taking the bull by the horns, coming right out and asking me. Without a second thought this time, I typed my reply, 'Ask away, Charlotte. No promises of any miracle cures, though. Log on to MSN Messenger so we can chat.'

And so began our relationship. Over the next week, Charlotte and I chatted online in the evenings for roughly half an hour at a time. She opened up her heart to me, pouring out torrents of misery in huge chunks, that both astounded and disturbed me.

It turned out that Jade had enrolled late into the same college as Charlotte, and had made it her job to make sure that every one of Charlotte's friends now avoided her and whispered loudly about her whenever she was around.

'But why would she do that?' I asked.

'Dunno. Because she can?' Charlotte replied miserably.

'Maybe she does it because she came here after us lot and it will get her in with the crowd quicker. Any way, it worked. She did it. Now she's in and I'm out.'

'What is she saying about you, exactly? Why can't you face up to her and have it out?'

'No one listens to me,' replied Charlotte. 'It's like I'm invisible. She accuses me of stuff, I deny it, they all laugh at me and walk away.'

I was puzzled. The very girls who used to be her friends were now turning on her. Why would they do that?

The next week, Charlotte came online mid-morning.

'What? No school?' I wrote.

'Period pains,' she replied.

Charlotte stayed at home for the rest of the week. The next week she went in on the Monday and then developed a bad migraine and stayed off for another couple of days.

We continued to chat, although college and friends were firmly off the agenda. I didn't ask too many questions, but listened very carefully. I was desperately trying to see beyond what she was saying. Charlotte had suddenly lost all her enthusiasm for college, yet had taken up an exhaustive exercise regime at home, clocking up ten kilometres on her mum's cross trainer every morning and evening and then spending time lifting dumbbells. This was the one thing that she could chat about with any enthusiasm. I decided we had built up sufficient trust by now for me to ask about the social situation at college.

'Has that boy asked you out yet?' I asked casually.

'Got to go, bad headache's coming on,' was the reply.

I sat staring at the screen. I knew she was lying. And she knew I knew.

Charlotte logged on for a chat later that evening, but I cried off, pretending I was busy. Maybe if she had to wait to talk to me, then she would spill everything out as soon as she got the chance. So I said I'd be free for a chat the next day.

'How's the head?'

'Better today. I managed thirteen kilometres this morning and did forty minutes' weights. My muscles are well toned.'

'No college?'

'End of term.'

Funny how quickly you lose track of term time as soon as you distance yourself from it. 'Sorry, I forgot.'

At a loss how to continue, I wrote, 'Lots of homework?'

'Not really. I'm thinking of giving it up anyway.'

Shocked, I tried to encourage her to open up. 'Not your sort of course after all?'

'It's not the course. It's other stuff. After what happened last month, my attendance has dropped right down. I'm in trouble with my teachers and my tutor, I'm falling behind and now Mum's started to wonder if I'm making excuses as well. Everyone's on my back and it's just getting worse.'

I had my suspicions and decided to voice them. 'Does this have anything to do with Jade, by any chance?'

'Jade's ruined my life. I hate her. You know that boy? He only came and sat down right opposite me on the same table in the canteen. He was dead nice, great blue eyes and black hair. Said his name was Craig and he'd seen me around. Asked me my name. Well, anyway, then he asked me out. Right there and then. Just came straight out with it. I was dead embarrassed, but I said, yes, I'd go to the cinema with him. Then, Jade walked up, pretended to slip and spilt her hot coffee all down me. It burnt my leg and hurt so much that I started to cry and ran out. I could hear her laughing. I was mortified. Then she came after me into the toilets and pushed my face right down into the toilet bowl. She told me to leave Craig alone, that he was spoken for. Or else. I was to keep my "fat fingers" off him, she said. After she'd gone, I stayed there for half an hour before daring to come out. Then I just ran home.'

'Jade's a rotten bully,' I wrote. 'Don't take any notice. Stand up to her. She'll move on to someone else then,' I said.

'It's not that easy,' Charlotte replied. 'After that, Jade and her other friends would wait until I'd got my food in the canteen, come up and pick fault with what I was eating. They whisper, "Fat bitch" at me in the corridor and say Craig must have been mad to look at a fat creep like me.'

I was confused. Charlotte wasn't fat at all; in fact she was more on the skinny side. 'Why on earth would they call you fat?' I asked.

Charlotte replied as if I hadn't interrupted. 'I know I'm fat, but I'll show them,' she continued.

'Charlotte, there are lots of things I could think of calling you, but "fat" isn't one of them,' I said. 'So what happened with Craig?'

'Jade took care of that. I'm not really sure what she told him, but it must have been bad, 'cos he cancelled the cinema with some lame excuse about having to baby-sit his little brother. Then he said he was well behind with his course-work, so it'd be better if we didn't see each other after all. Kelly's going out with him now. Kelly, of all people. She used to be my friend. She hangs onto his arm the whole day, staring up at him. She makes me sick. They both do.'

I didn't know what to say to make her feel any better. She was certainly having a rotten time of it. 'It seems to me your work is suffering because of all this, Charlotte,' I said. 'And then Jade will have won. You were always hard-working and proud of your achievements. Are you going to let her do this to you? Are you going to let her bully you into failing?'

'No. Yes. Well, I don't want to fall behind. But I can't go to college. I really do get headaches, you know, and I've developed this bad cough as well. When I'm back at home, I can relax and concentrate on exercising. That makes me feel in control of things again.'

'Have you told your mum any of this?' I asked, knowing what the answer would be.

My heart sank as she replied, 'No way. I'll never tell anyone. Ever.'

The signs were there; I made the mistake of misreading them. Charlotte had entrusted me with her deepest feelings.

I was in the unique position of being able to try and help her. And I bungled it.

For my part, I didn't speak about my relationship with Charlotte to anyone, not even my husband, Ben. He was used to me replying to emails and conversing with strangers, and therefore unaware of the intensity of this particular relationship. So I found myself in turmoil over deciding how to intervene. Ben and I usually discuss all our worries, yet in this instance, I felt it would be inappropriate and unfair to Charlotte.

Home alone with my thoughts, I ran a bath, adding extra bubble bath. Sinking beneath the bubbles, I closed my eyes and mentally put myself into Charlotte's shoes. 'Okay, I am Charlotte. What makes me feel good? Well, home is where I feel safe. Exercise gives me control. Mrs Trevane trusts me. That's about it.'

Then I thought about the things that made her feel bad, and there was a frighteningly long list: Jade, her new-found friends-turned-enemies, Craig, college, Mum, headaches. Charlotte was living increasingly as a recluse, not enjoying any of the social things a normal, healthy teenager did. She was generally alone and sad, invisible to the rest of the world. I was the only one she had turned to. I had to do something. But what?

As far as I could see, Charlotte was steadily sinking into depression, while I sat and watched. Listening in vain to her cries for help was no longer enough. It was time for some action. Time to involve other people to build up a support group for Charlotte. I hoped she'd agree with my decision. I decided to start by encouraging her to talk to her parents. After careful consideration, I took the plunge and sat at the computer.

'Okay, Charlotte, here's my first suggestion,' I wrote. 'Find a time when your mum and dad can both give you their undivided attention. Sit down together, turn off the TV and tell them why you are unhappy. You'll probably be pleasantly surprised at their reaction.'

'Somehow I don't think so,' came the reply. 'Dad upped and left last Christmas. Said he couldn't pretend any more. Playing "happy families" was doing his head in, he said. Went to live with a slapper he met down the pub. Only twenty-two she is. He's forty-three. I think it's disgusting. Now Mum cries a lot and drinks too much at weekends and goes on and on to me about if I'd been easier to handle he'd never have left.'

My God! Poor Charlotte. How naïve and stupid of me to assume things were hunky-dory at home. Here she was, crying out for help, advice and attention. Instead, she was becoming increasingly weighed down by the pressure on her to support her mum, as well as taking the blame for her parents' split. She must be devastated. No wonder she felt she couldn't turn to her mum. That would make her into even more of a burden.

'I bet her mum has no idea of the turmoil Charlotte's going through,' I thought to myself. 'She'll be completely oblivious to the damage being done.'

'Would you consider talking to your doctor?' I asked. 'You're sixteen, so no one else would have to know. Who is your doctor?'

'We're registered with the village practice, so any of them really – if I ever have an appointment, I just make it with whoever's available,' answered Charlotte.

This sounded encouraging. 'So is there a female doctor there?' I asked.

'Dr Turnbull. She's okay.'

I stumbled on, hoping she'd go through with it. 'How about it, then? You don't have to tell her anything you don't want to. She's in a much better position to offer you help, and she's a professional.'

'Do you want me to stop chatting to you?'

I winced at Charlotte's reply. She certainly was a sensitive one. 'That's not what I meant. You can chat to me as much as you like. But chat to Dr Turnbull as well. See what happens.'

Silence.

After a couple of minutes, I tried again. 'If it doesn't work out, then don't go back. What have you got to lose?'

'Okay, I'll make an appointment.'

I needed to push for more. 'Today?'

'Today.'

I went to bed that night praying that Charlotte would be able to find some hope from her doctor. 'Please show her compassion,' I prayed. If the doctor could help Charlotte to see that she didn't have to face things alone, she'd have a half-decent chance of recovery. She had to start believing that it was not all her fault.

The next evening, I logged on early, anxious to know how she'd got on.

'Well, how did it go?'

Charlotte replied straightaway. 'It was okay. Listen, could I ask you a big favour? Would you meet me in town tomorrow morning? We could go for a coffee and have a proper chat. Then I can tell you exactly what happened.'

I had a mountain of work, a couple of important calls to make and a hair appointment planned for then. I couldn't possibly fit her in.

'Course I can, Charlotte. I'll meet you outside Starbucks at ten-thirty.'

She was late. At ten-forty-five, I decided to have a coffee anyway. I ordered a cappuccino, and gingerly sipped it through the froth, trying not to get a moustache in the process. I ran my fingers through my hair, which had become annoyingly messy. 'I could be being pampered in the hair salon at this very moment, if I hadn't cancelled,' I thought, closing my eyes to imagine the scene.

'Hello, Mrs Trevane. Sorry I'm late.'

I opened my eyes and looked up to see Charlotte standing shyly by the table. 'Hi there,' I smiled. 'Let me get you a coffee or something.' I started to get up. 'Would you like a cake or a pastry to go with it?' I asked.

Putting out her hand, Charlotte stopped me. 'Oh, no, please don't get up. I'll get the coffee.'

I watched her approach the counter and stand in the queue. She was a shadow of her former self. Her long hair had lost its lustre and her coat hung on her. 'She must have lost around twenty pounds,' I thought. 'And she was thin to start with. She looks dreadful.'

Charlotte, however, returned with the coffee smiling broadly. 'It's so good to see you again,' she said.

Despite my secret horror at her outward appearance, her mood was infectious and I smiled back. 'You too,' I said. I extended my hand, took her own and squeezed it, noticing the chewed, red fingers as I did so.

That was all the encouragement she needed. With a sip of her coffee, she rambled happily on about the meeting with the doctor. By the time she'd finished, I was in need of another drink. Charlotte's cup was still full.

'The great thing is, she seemed really interested,' continued Charlotte. 'She wants me to speak to another lady, a counsellor, though. This Tuesday. I'm not sure about that.'

'Take things one at a time,' I advised her. 'See the doctor, take the tablets and then, if you're strong enough, consider counselling. That's the whole point of all this, Charlotte. You're in charge here. It's what you want, when you want, and only if you want it.'

By the time we said our goodbyes, Charlotte was in high spirits. She gave me a quick hug and disappeared into the crowds. I stayed behind for another coffee. Would the antidepressants help? Yes, of course they would. That's what was wrong. And now it was sorted.

The next evening, Charlotte logged in as usual for our chat.

'I feel so much more hopeful,' she wrote. 'Maybe I will see the counsellor lady after all.'

Things were definitely looking up.

'That's good,' I replied. 'What about college? Do you think you can face it?'

'I keep getting the headaches,' replied Charlotte. 'I don't know if I can face Craig yet. I still like him, you know.'

'Is he still with Kelly?' I asked.

'That didn't last two minutes. I haven't been to college for a while, so I don't know if he's seeing anyone else. Probably is. Someone thin and pretty, I expect. All I know is, it's not me. And never will be. It's all about physical appearance and image these days.'

I pictured her bitten fingers, baggy clothes, pinched face and gaunt eyes. 'Well if it is, you're not trying very hard in the competition stakes,' I thought to myself.

I remembered her exercise routine. 'How's the training?' I asked. 'Are you super fit yet?'

'I'm still building it up. Some days I get up at night to do a kilometre and fifty press-ups and then go back to bed.'

It didn't add up. If she was working herself so hard, then why wasn't she a glowing picture of health?

'Why do you push yourself so hard?' I wrote.

'Every time she sees me, she taunts me constantly about being fat,' came the reply. 'I'll show her.'

My heart sank. 'Jade?'

'I exercise every spare moment until my whole body is screaming,' she went on. 'For a while, I feel better, like I've regained control, but when I wake up, the horrid feelings are right back again. My head aches and I always feel so weak. She makes me feel ugly and worthless.'

'You're not ugly or worthless,' I said. 'You have a pretty face, beautiful wavy hair, and a great body.'

'Jade's right. I am fat,' was the reply. 'I know it. I'm in control, though.'

'Charlotte, have you put yourself on a diet?' I asked. 'You looked as if you'd lost weight when I saw you.'

'I've lost some, but it's not enough. I bulge out everywhere. If I think about Jade, I feel so bad. I drop my calorie intake and increase my work-outs. I want to be at least as thin as her.'

Jade was about a size twelve. I guessed that Charlotte had started out as that, but was now a size eight. 'But you're much slimmer than Jade,' I said.

'Don't flatter me, Mrs Trevane. I might have taken the mirror out of my bedroom, but I know if I'm fat or not. And I'm not just fat, I'm disgusting.'

There was no point in trying to convince her otherwise. She obviously had low self-esteem and all this was part of it. The tablets should help.

'Look,' I said. 'You've been really brave and taken that first step to see a doctor. Now what about your future? You can't stay away from college forever. You need to think seriously about what you want. Do you want to carry on and work hard? Or throw in the towel, because a girl is giving you a hard time?'

'She's making my life hell,' said Charlotte. 'When I'm at home, I think I can handle her. But I can't really. I'm safe at home. At college, all the feelings come back and I can't cope. I can't face my tutor either. I've never been a shirker before, and I'm so ashamed. What would I say to explain my bad attendance?'

'Why don't you write to him?' I suggested. 'That way, you can plan out everything you say, and you won't be put on the spot. Plus it gives you a chance to explain everything in the way you want.'

'Okay, I'll give it a try, but I'll see this lady first,' said Charlotte.

The counsellor was a godsend. Not only did she reinforce the idea that what Charlotte had to say was important; she also gave her the confidence to write to the college, outlining the personal circumstances responsible for her absence and requesting a meeting to arrange catch-up sessions.

Between the doctor, the counsellor and myself, Charlotte had a mini network of support for the first time, which seemed to be having a positive effect. She managed to arrange for extra tutorials, and got permission to work at home for four days a week, agreeing to attend on Thursdays. I made sure that we chatted every Wednesday evening, to bolster her up enough to face college the next day.

This went on for five weeks. Charlotte worked hard at home, anxious to do well and get the grades she deserved.

She pored over books and managed to hand in two long essays by the end of the second week. She saw the counsellor every Tuesday for an hour, and the doctor every three weeks.

Thursdays were obviously difficult for her. I always tried to ask her about the day – what she had for lunch among other things. She always replied that she never ate at college, as it would just give Jade something to shout about or find fault with.

I then noticed that, on Thursdays, Charlotte would only chat for ten minutes, saying she had to go out for a power walk before it got dark. It was as if her exercise regime was becoming increasingly compulsive.

Then, in the sixth week after her return to college, she logged on and wrote the words, 'I can't go on.'

'What is it? What's happened?' I asked, dreading the answer and assuming it would concern Jade.

'It's all my fault. If I hadn't caused so many arguments at home, Dad would never have left and then all this would never have happened. I just want to die.'

I knew Charlotte only saw her dad one weekend in every month. 'Did he cancel or something?' I asked.

'No. But I didn't stay. I couldn't. Not after what he's done.'

I was still completely in the dark. 'What's happened?'

'He's only gone and got her pregnant, that's what. And they're keeping it. And he's only asked her to marry him. He's not even divorced yet, for God's sake.'

'Charlotte, none of this is your fault. Don't be silly,' I

said, trying to make her feel better. I should have been more careful with my choice of words.

'Silly? That's what *he* called me, when I ran off. So now, even you think I'm being silly? Well, maybe I am. Silly to be upset when your dad throws away one family and starts another, and silly to think you'd ever believe in me. Got to go now.'

I thought quickly. It was Monday. She had an appointment with Dr Turnbull in an hour, and she was due to see the counsellor the following day. They should be able to help. I decided to leave things to them. Better to give her space and time to calm down.

By Tuesday evening, I had convinced myself that it was pointless worrying, when there were two professionals on call. I waited for Charlotte to contact me. Sure enough, at our time of seven o'clock, she wrote, 'I'm such a failure.'

I stared at her words. 'Why do you think that?'

'Dr Turnbull weighed me. She's got these weird digital scales that are supposed to be accurate. But they're not. Apparently, I weigh seven and a half stone. But I know I only weigh seven stone six. Those scales are ridiculous. How can I have put on a pound? A whole pound? I'm so overweight, but she told me I had to put some weight on! I'm definitely not going to see her again.'

'Oh, Charlotte, seven and a half stone? How can you even imagine you're overweight?' I asked. 'You're quite tall too, about five feet seven, so that weight isn't nearly enough.'

'Nobody understands,' she said. 'I thought I could easily

control my weight loss. But it seems that I can't even do that.'

She *was* being silly now, I thought. How could she think that she was fat, when all she had to do was look in the mirror? I decided to change the subject. 'How's the work going?'

'Got one of my essays back today. Only got a B. I worked so hard on it to get an A. Everything's going wrong. Can't chat now. My head's splitting and I need to exercise. Bye.'

After that conversation, our relationship began to change, as Charlotte gradually withdrew back into herself. Half-hourly chats became twenty minutes and eventually ten, and then only two or three times a week. She was no longer willing to express her feelings, choosing to clam up and change the subject. It was as if I was losing her. She stopped going to college on Thursdays and became a virtual recluse. Her mum was drinking more and more, which gave Charlotte the perfect excuse to stay at home, to watch over her.

Two months later, Charlotte stopped chatting to me. I logged on each evening, I sent emails, but she didn't reply. After a week had gone by with no word from her, a nagging worry drove me to look up her phone number and ring her. I just needed to know that she was okay.

'Hello?'

It wasn't Charlotte's voice. 'Mrs Borman? My name is Jacky Trevane. I used to teach your daughter, Charlotte. Could I speak to her please?'

I felt guilty for some reason. Suddenly I knew why. In that moment, I realised that Charlotte and I had conducted all of our relationship behind this woman's back. Her own mother knew nothing about me. I felt as if I had deceived her. And now it was too late to try and explain. She would never understand.

'I'm afraid you can't. She's not here. She collapsed, you see, and they took her to hospital. On a drip to make her eat. Silly girl. As if I don't cook decent meals. There's always good food to be had in this house . . .'

As she rambled on, my mind was in a whirl. Drip? Not eating? Collapsed? The poor girl was anorexic. It had been staring me in the face all this time, and I just hadn't seen it. It was now so obvious it could have blinded me. How could I have not recognised the signs? All that exercise, the headaches, the excuses not to eat.

'. . . I'm sorry, what did you say your name was again?'

'Jacky,' I answered. 'Jacky Trevane. If it's all right with you, Mrs Borman, I'd like to visit Charlotte. Which ward is she in, please?'

She was sleeping. The sight of her lying in bed, her body hardly making an impression in the sheets, with her pale little face on the pillow, was heart-wrenching. She was a pathetic sight. I looked at her records at the end of the bed. Weight: 41 kg; about six and a half stone. I sat beside the bed and took her bony hand. She stirred.

'Hi, Charlotte, what are we going to do with you?' I smiled. She turned to face me and smiled weakly back. 'I'm sorry.

I can't do this any more. All I do is cause problems for everyone.'

'You're not causing anyone problems. But you're not doing yourself any good either,' I said. 'Surely you can see that? Your body needs food to keep you going.'

'Yes, but when I step on those scales and they tell me I've lost weight, it makes me feel so good. I know it's bad, but I want that feeling. It gives me such a buzz. Like the exercise. I feel great afterwards. It's almost trance-like. Whenever I eat, I feel guilty. So I get into the habit of not eating anything, burning off calories with exercise, and making sure everyone thinks I'm eating properly.' She looked away and lowered her voice. 'Do you remember when I told you I used to get up in the night to exercise?'

'I remember.'

'Well, I used to wake up because of these awful hunger pains. They made me double up. I could have eaten a horse. I did the exercise to take my mind off it and wear me out so that I could get back to sleep.'

'Charlotte, can you hear yourself? Can you really hear what you are saying? If you carry on like that, it won't be a hospital bed you'll end up in, it'll be a coffin.' I raised my voice. 'And I'm not joking, young lady. This is your life you're playing with.'

A tear dripped down her cheek. 'I know that. But at the moment, the two most important things in my life are losing weight and exercise. It's absolute hell.'

I stayed for an hour, desperately trying to convince her

how different things could be if she could find the strength to take charge of her life in a different way. When I left, I felt drained and helpless. I hadn't helped her at all. I promised to visit again, went home and finally poured out my heart to Ben, telling him the whole story. It had been a very long day.

Charlotte was eventually discharged from hospital. Since then, she has been readmitted twice. Her weight fluctuates between underweight and dangerously underweight. Her condition, now recognised and out in the open, has shocked her mum into doing something about her own problems, and she is now making a real effort to help Charlotte. The hospital are involved, as are counsellors, and her weight is monitored on a regular basis. Yet it seems to be an uphill struggle for her. One step forward, two back. She turned to me and I misread the signals. I let her down.

Charlotte recently described her life to me as she saw it. This is what she said, 'My life is a living hell, a complete nightmare. The only difference is, I will never wake up.'

15

Shy Girl

Having escaped from Egypt and the horrors that occurred there, it took quite a while for me to build a new life for my two daughters and me. These days, I rarely speak about the nightmares I still have, the looking over my shoulder, the screaming, panicky feeling inside me whenever I recall those bad times. In fact, I never talk about it. I just live with it. This is me now. On the outside, I am a regular mum from the north of England, like any other. I never stopped to think that there were probably lots of 'regular' mums who had suffered just like me, who were also keeping it all inside. The more people I speak to, the more I realise that there are women everywhere living 'regular' lives, hiding their suffering of one form or another. Every so often, something happens to remind me of this.

Not long ago, I gave a talk about my book, *Fatwa*, to a lovely group of ladies from the NHR, National House-wives Register. They gave me a very warm reception, and the evening was a great success. The following week, Joan, the hostess, telephoned me to ask if I would visit her friend, Margaret, whose daughter had gone through similar experiences to mine, as described in *Fatwa*.

'She didn't come to the talk, but when I heard you speaking of your experiences, I immediately thought about Margaret,' Joan explained. 'She's never spoken about her daughter much, but from what I can gather, she married a Moslem and had a tough time of it. Anyway, I lent her my copy of *Fatwa*. She read it in a couple of days and phoned me straightaway to ask if she could meet you. Very emotional, she sounded.'

'I'd be happy to talk to her,' I replied. 'What's her number?'

'I rather think she wants to meet you,' said Joan.

It was something of a shock for me to hear that Margaret lived in the same village as my parents when they were alive. The village where I had grown up and gone to school. The village that I had left to go to university, and then to work in the south of England, and finally to live in Egypt. The village that I had returned to with my daughters.

Since my Egyptian husband issued the fatwa on me, we have changed our names four times and moved house five. We therefore no longer live in the village. I phoned Margaret and agreed to drive over and meet her. It felt strange, almost too close for comfort; me returning to my roots to hear about another girl from the same village, who had endured pain and suffering similar to my own.

I pulled into the driveway and was locking the car, when the door of the house opened and a tall lady with shoulder-length, blonde hair stepped out to greet me. Smartly dressed in a flattering skirt and jumper, she shook my hand warmly and introduced herself as Margaret.

I walked into the immaculately furnished lounge and glanced out of the window into the garden. It was a bright morning, although still cold. Spring was in the air and the sun was shining onto the bench in front of a summerhouse.

'What a lovely garden,' I said, smiling. There were two levels, a beautifully designed patio, leading down to lawn and a rockery, with borders and shrubs in pots dotted around. A summerhouse was to one side, facing south, and they had made a feature of a tree, with a miniature wall and white gravel surrounding it.

'Andrew and I love it,' said Margaret, joining me at the window. 'We've put in a lot of effort to get it exactly how we want it. We only moved here last September, so we've done quite well in seven months.'

With a sigh, she turned away. A graceful, gentle woman in her sixties, Margaret's voice was soft, yet tinged with resolution. She moved across the room and sat on one of the huge brown sofas. I sat opposite her expectantly.

'Thank you for coming,' she began. 'Your book struck a lot of familiar chords with me. I read it in a couple of days but, to be honest, some of the scenes you describe are exactly how I'd imagined things to be with my daughter. I read and reread those pages, crying a little and eventually sobbing my heart out. In all these years, I have told no one the whole story. I have kept everything locked away in here.' She patted her chest. 'It was all so terrible, I thought no one would believe me, or really understand. Until I read your book. You will be the first person to hear the full story in thirty years.

'Nicola was eighteen when she first met him. It must have been in 1975. She had received her diploma for hairdressing and beauty at college and was working in a local hairdressing salon. She wanted to do the course for gents' hair, in order to open her own unisex hair salon eventually, so she enrolled for the course. Karim was the model she practised on. At the time, she was living at home with us and our three other daughters, aged fifteen, thirteen and eleven. Anyway, they started to spend a lot of time together, although she never mentioned him to us. We knew absolutely nothing about him, or even that she was seeing someone on a regular basis. If she went out, she would simply tell us she was going out with her friends. She was a good girl, always coming in at a reasonable hour. We had no reason to suspect she was hiding anything from us.'

Margaret paused and clamped her lips together, as if the memory was painful to her. I sat quietly, not wanting to disturb the mood. With a sigh, she continued, 'My husband and I were both lecturers at the college and knew most of the staff. We were friendly with the foreign liaison officer, Bob, whose job it was to monitor the integration of foreign students into the community and their attendance on the courses, etc. Anyway, he telephoned us one evening – as a friend, you understand,' she added. 'He said he was a little concerned that Nicola was spending a lot of time with Karim and that they were canoodling in public, obviously having a relationship. I was surprised to hear this, as Nicky hadn't mentioned having a steady boyfriend, but not unduly worried. Nicky would tell us when she was ready, I thought. I was about to reassure Bob not to worry, when he added something that changed everything. He said that Karim was a student from Libya and had married an English girl in the town, who was now pregnant with their first child.

'We confronted Nicky that day, who swept all our concerns under the carpet. Yes, she was seeing a student from Libya, but his name wasn't Karim, it was Magdi. And no, he wasn't married, so we hadn't to worry.'

Margaret shrugged. 'We believed her, of course. It's easy to believe what you want to when the alternative is unsavoury. We assumed Bob had got his wires crossed, and thought no more about it. A couple of weeks later, Bob called again, voicing the same concerns. He said he was sure Nicky was seeing Karim, not Magdi. He didn't know of a student called Magdi. He reeled off Karim's full name and gave the address where he was living with his wife. All we could do was thank him and say we would take it further.

'That evening, Andrew asked Nicky where she was going,' Margaret continued. 'When she said she was going to the King's Head for a meal with Magdi, we smiled and waved her off. As soon as she'd left, we showered and changed and went off to confront them. I was shaking inside and very nervous. Andrew did all the talking. He strode up to their table and without introduction, accused Magdi of being an imposter. He reeled off Karim's full name, address and put in the extra fact of having a pregnant wife.'

A tear rolled down her cheek.

'What happened?' I asked, prompting her to continue.

'Well, nothing went as I'd expected,' she said, wiping away the tear. 'Nicky didn't look at all shocked, merely embarrassed. She put her head down and said nothing. It dawned on me that she had known all along. Karim waited for Andrew to stop ranting, smiled, stood up and tried to shake his hand. He was charming. So charming. Immaculately dressed. Stunning to look at. His English accent was impeccable. I could see in an instant why Nicky had fallen for him. He persuaded us to join them at the table and, within half an hour, had convinced us that he had not lived with his wife for five months, that he loved Nicky and didn't want to hurt our feelings. It all seems so unlikely now,' she added. 'But at the time, he was extremely plausible and convincing. We came away with our tails between our legs.

'That's how it all began, really,' she continued with a sigh. 'I started noticing little things at home that weren't quite right; the kettle would be warm when we returned from work, or sometimes I could have sworn that a chair had been moved, or a towel was in a different place. It turned out that Karim had used Nicky's key to let himself into our house every day after we'd all left for work. He'd spend the day there and leave before we arrived home. When the truth dawned, we were not best pleased, obviously. But Nicky's attitude was to defend Karim's actions, saying he had nowhere else to go. It seemed to have escaped her notice that, although he was spending the days at our house, he continued to sleep at his other house with his pregnant wife.

'Anyway, the upshot of all this was that Nicky announced that she was moving out, into a flat with Karim. She was looking at hair salons in a town about thirty miles away, where they were cheaper. The plan was to open a hair and beauty salon and live nearby. Initially they put a deposit down on a newbuild, but then found a salon with a flat above it and decided to move there instead.' She turned to me and raised her voice slightly. 'Can you believe it? This "wonderful" man, with whom my daughter was in love, moved out of his house on the very day that his wife went into labour. Now that's what I call wonderful,' she said, her voice dripping with sarcasm. 'What sort of person would do that?'

'That's terrible,' I said.

'I tried talking sense into her. I tried to make her see that he had a ruthless side to him. I said, if he was so wonderful, why would he be so callous as to leave his wife in the lurch when she was giving birth to his first child? He was selfish, I said. "At the moment he wants you, Nicky, so he's showing you his charming side. But what will happen when he tires of you and wants someone else?"' She wrung her hands together. 'But of course she didn't listen. Actually, she laughed and told me I was being silly to worry. She moved out the next week.'

'That must have been an emotional day for you,' I said.

'Oh, yes. But Nicky was determined. And where Karim was concerned, she was adamant that they would be together forever. This was it, she said. The big one. She was infatuated.'

Margaret stared out onto the garden. I had a lump in my throat. It was as if she was my own mother, sitting there looking lost, gazing into the distance. I remembered the time when I had sat with my parents and told them that I had met the love of my life and I was going to live with him. Whatever they said, however rational their objections, I had an answer. Just like Nicky. This was it. The big one. I was determined, and nothing they could say was going to put me off.

Only now, in this sitting-room on this bright, spring morning, watching the pain etched on Margaret's face as she remembered, was I able to finally see how deeply hurt and bewildered my own parents must have been. The realisation had come far too late, however; I had been too consumed with passion and completely wrapped up in my own future to think of their feelings. And I could also see how it must have been for Margaret and Andrew. Desperate. Hopeless. Helpless.

I felt quite sick. I wanted to rush up to my mum and dad, wrap my arms around them and try and make them feel better. But of course I couldn't. They were both dead now. For me it was too late.

But surely not for Margaret and Andrew? After all, Nicky was only moving a few miles away, and all children fly the nest at some stage in their lives. It wasn't as if she was following him to Libya or anything. Merely an hour's drive away. Why was she so sad?

'My parents went through hell when I ran off to Egypt,' I said. 'At the time, I didn't focus on how they must have been feeling. But you've made me see how they suffered.'

Margaret was miles away, locked in a private reverie. My words jolted her back to the present. She smiled a wry smile. 'You have no idea,' she replied. 'I think we lost our daughter the day she moved out of the family home. She was besotted with Karim, and working all hours of the day and night. After hours, Libyan women would go to the salon to have their hair or nails done. She was very good at fancy manicures and pedicures. They kept themselves to themselves pretty much. Karim was reluctant for her to have much to do with us, although when we did meet, he was as charming as ever. He always insisted on cooking, and would present us with some lavish spread, a feast in fact. He was careful to be respectful and polite, chatting as if we were very close. But there were never opportunities for Nicky and me to be alone together, to go shopping, or meet up for lunch or coffee. She was always working, or *he* was there, supervising everything. Even at Christmas, we would only see them for a few hours.'

I was intrigued. 'If Nicky was working all the time, what did Karim do?' I asked.

'Well, that's anyone's guess,' said Margaret. 'He was enrolled on a degree course in engineering, up north, but never seemed to do a scrap of work for it. He was always popping off up there for a few days to do a bit of "business" here and a bit there. He never said exactly and we never knew. Nicky refused to be drawn on the subject. She wouldn't hear a word said against Karim, and it was difficult enough talking to her when he wasn't there. But he never seemed to do anything at all.

'Life carried on like this for quite a few years,' Margaret said. 'The business flourished, and they bought three terraced houses. The plan was for my dad, who's a builder, and Karim to renovate them and let them out. The reality was that my dad did 90 per cent of the renovations and Karim dipped his finger in occasionally and charmed his way out of putting in any useful contribution to the project. Then they bought a lovely house to live in, and rented out the flat above the salon. Despite our feelings towards Karim, we were so proud of Nicky and what she'd managed to achieve. She now employed other hairdressers and a manageress at the salon, although she still put in the hours herself too.'

I thought of my own situation in Egypt. Certain similarities were beginning to emerge. It was strange, but my husband, Omar, had also done a little bit of this and a little bit of that to earn money, while I had the steady teaching job and the private lessons in the evening that had brought us virtually everything we owned.

'Did they ever marry?' I asked.

'Eventually, yes,' she replied. 'They'd been together for

about ten years, when Nicky told me she was going to convert to Islam, cover her head, and marry Karim in a mosque. We were horrified. We are Christians, and it's all we've ever known. We couldn't agree with this turn of events at all. I begged her to reconsider and have a civil ceremony here instead. It was the first time for years I'd ever voiced a strong opinion, but apparently it had the desired effect. They agreed to marry here at the registry office. We were over the moon.'

I laughed. 'I bet you were,' I said. 'I didn't understand a thing at my wedding. It all went completely over my head.'

'It was a lovely day,' Margaret continued. 'The odd thing though, was that there was no one there to represent Karim. No family members, nor a single friend. We found out later that he hadn't told anyone about it. The following month, they went down to London, unbeknown to us and married in a lavish Moslem ceremony. We weren't invited. All his family and relations flew in for it. As far as they were concerned, their darling son was getting married for the first time. He was a sly one, that Karim. His first wife had also been called Nicky, and he was able to charm his way out of many awkward explanations. How's that for a coincidence?'

Margaret shrugged. 'Anyway, if we thought we'd lost our daughter the day she moved out, then we'd certainly lost her the day she married Karim. He changed overnight, and her with him.'

'Why am I not surprised?' I thought. The charm is in the

chase until the ring goes on the finger. Then you're his. 'What happened?' I asked.

'First, Nicky converted to Islam. She wore long clothes and covered her head at all times. She never actually told me; suddenly she was too busy to see me, or she'd agree for me to visit and then cancel. So it must have been six months after their marriage before I saw her. Usually she greeted me at the door with a hug and a smile. On this occasion, Karim was waiting at the gate, and ushered me in quickly. Nicky was waiting quietly in the sitting-room. I was shocked at the change that had come over her. Head bowed, she only spoke if spoken to by Karim and seemed at a loss to know what to say to me. In stark contrast, Karim was being his usual charming self, witty, gregarious, engaging as ever. It was Karim who informed me of their Moslem wedding and Nicky's conversion to Islam. This was an awful lot for me to take in. I became increasingly bewildered and confused, as he paraded a couple of wedding photographs in front of me and animatedly described the no-expense-spared long weekend.

'Her name was no longer Nicky, but Amal now, he said. I was horrified and looked over questioningly at Nicky. Surely she would put me out of my misery and explain? She said nothing, her eyes never leaving Karim's face as he walked round the room, watching him speak adoringly and nodding in agreement to everything he said. When she looked at me, her eyes were blank, no longer smiling from within. I tried to hug her, but she shrugged me off and turned away. I was aching to ask her what had happened, but it was awkward with Karim breathing down my neck. I took a chance and whispered that I would come to see her at the salon, but she didn't respond. As I was leaving, under Karim's insistent escort of course, he proudly informed me that my daughter was five months pregnant. I had no chance to say anything to Nicky; he had already ushered me out of the door.

'After that I was no longer welcome at the house. The reason he gave was because I didn't wear a veil or long skirts to cover my modesty. He said it was his religion, but I know he was just using that as an excuse. Moslem families are perfectly entitled to mix with people of other religions, aren't they?'

'Of course they are,' I replied. 'Islam is actually a wonderful religion, if it is respected and followed in a rational way.'

Margaret looked surprised to hear me say this. 'But I thought you hated Moslems,' she said. 'In your book, your husband did all those things to you and he was a Moslem.'

'My story was just that,' I replied. 'A personal experience. Omar was a selfish man who manipulated his religion and used it to abuse me. I don't blame the religion. I blame him. The funny thing is, I've never read the Bible from cover to cover, but I've read the Qu'ran. I was given an English translation, a huge book, when I converted, and I spent many hours poring over it. It's inspiring, and I've since met Moslem couples who are great examples of the true meaning of Islam. But it's also frightening to admit that there are a lot of Omars out there, who control their wives totally and beat them regularly on the premise that they have sinned or disobeyed them as decreed in the Qu'ran. It's just not true; nowhere in this great book does it say that the man controls his wife and can beat her, yet so many do it and get away with it.'

'He got away with murder,' she whispered.

I leaned forward. 'Sorry, Margaret, I didn't catch that. What did you say?'

She didn't reply. Instead, she returned to her story. 'I was at a loss to know what to do. We both were. Andrew knew that to confront Karim would be useless; he had an answer for everything and we were no longer fooled by his smiles and hollow explanations. Was he hitting her? We needed to try and reach Nicky and get to the bottom of things. I decided to visit the salon. When I arrived, she was cutting a customer's hair and refused to take time out to speak to me. Even in her long clothes, I could see that she had visibly lost weight and was painfully thin. She begged me to leave and I was about to comply, when suddenly all the anger and frustration inside me bubbled over. I grabbed her arm and hissed into her ear, "Something's not right, Nicky, and I'm going to get to the bottom of this." I was shaking with anger, but she merely moved away from my grasp, with the reply, "My name's Amal." There was nothing we could do. Absolutely nothing. I felt as if I had lost my daughter.'

Wiping the tears from her eyes with her hand, Margaret got up to get a tissue. 'Over the next few years, we hardly saw them. It broke my heart. Nicky gave birth to a little boy,

Mahmoud, and eighteen months later she had a daughter, Latifa. In four years we must have seen them only a handful of times. Lovely children, but they never knew us as Nanny and Grandad. Nicky doted on the children and continued to work long hours. Yet not once did she contact us, ring us up to say hello, or bring the children to visit. I kept trying to see them, but in vain.

'It must have been about three years after their marriage when they went to stay in a flat up north, while Karim went to university to catch up on his studies. He got himself into a spot of bother with the authorities over deadlines, and thought nothing of contacting me to ask me to visit his tutor and ask for more time for him to complete his assignments. I know it sounds unbelievable now, sitting here,' she said, 'but at the time, he was so polite and the way he put it was so plausible that I agreed to travel up and see what I could do. He said Nicky was in a very fragile state of mind and needed a lot of looking after. His request meant, of course, that I would get the chance to see my daughter and grandchildren for a few days, so I was glad for an excuse to visit. It was wonderful to see them. I did as I'd promised, visited Karim's tutor, and convinced him to give him a decent extension, citing Nicky's condition as the main reason for his lack of work so far.

'Karim was right; Nicky was jumpy, nervous and reluctant to go out. She told me some very strange things, which I assumed was all in her imagination. I tried to make light of her claims that Karim was trying to send her insane by

175

making her believe that his dead father was visiting her every night at the foot of the bed, wearing long, white robes. She also said she had been brutally raped by three men while Karim watched. I had been awake for most of the night, and would have heard any untoward activity. I assumed Nicky was imagining it. I did notice, however, that Karim's tone changed when he addressed her; he ordered her around and bullied her constantly, although with me he couldn't have been more charming. Her reaction was always to submit, never argue back. Every day, he would get angry with Nicky over something, and frequently bring up the subject of the children. He would threaten to take them away if she couldn't show herself to be a good mother. This was his real power over Nicky. She lived in fear of losing the children. She had these long, wide, crepe bandages, which she wound around herself and then around the children each night, so that they were bound together. Otherwise, she couldn't sleep, afraid that Karim might take them away and she wouldn't know about it.'

Margaret sighed. 'She was on the edge, mentally. During the night, she would cry out or scream in her sleep. It was very disturbing to me. The first night, I rushed into her room and lay with her on the bed until Karim came up. He was not amused to find me there, so I decided to stay in my room after that. The next night, however, I was on my way to the bathroom, when I caught Karim coming quietly up the stairs, dressed in a long, white sheet. Nicky hadn't been dreaming, I realised. I challenged him, angrily accusing him of trying to send Nicky mad, but he merely laughed in my face.

'I sat with Nicky the next day, trying to make her see how unhealthy her relationship with Karim was, and begging her to see sense and leave him, but she wouldn't hear of it. It was obvious that I had outstayed my welcome. I decided to ring Andrew and tell him to meet me off the train. They didn't have a phone at the flat, and it was in the days before mobile phones. The weather had turned cold and I had brought only a light jacket with me, so I borrowed Nicky's thick, black overcoat and set off to walk to the nearest phone box. On the way, a white van stopped by the kerb. Three men leered out at me, asking if I'd enjoyed it and that they were definitely returning soon for second helpings. As I turned to face them, they realised I wasn't Nicky. The driver put his foot down and they screeched away into the distance. Two of the men were white and one black. Shaking, I made the call to Andrew and returned to the flat to ask Nicky about the van. It belonged to the men who lived next door, she said. There were three of them. The three who had raped her.

'Listening to her words for the second time, I realised with horror that she had been telling the truth. I had to do something. Knowing that Karim was very adept at manip- ulating angry women, I took a different tack, suggesting I took Nicky and the children back to their family house, while he finished his assignment. It wouldn't take him half as long, I reasoned, and then he could be back with them sooner. He saw the sense of my suggestion, and so we all travelled back the next day. Despite me asking Nicky about her ordeal, she now clammed up, asking me to leave. Without her support, I couldn't progress things any further.

'Once again, she never phoned, visited or invited us over,' Margaret continued sadly. 'Karim returned and the silence between us reigned. One day, I decided to take my chances and drive to the house to see if Karim would send me away, or if he'd be charming and let me in. At least I'd set eyes on Nicky. I took a food parcel with me. When I arrived, no one was in, so I left the food at the back door. I returned the next week to find the food exactly where I had left it. Fortunately, a neighbour was able to tell me that they'd gone to Libya for a holiday for two months. I was devastated to think that she couldn't even have been bothered enough to pick up the phone and tell me they were going. It was like a bad dream.

'It was all becoming too much for me to bear,' Margaret continued. I returned to work that week, sick with worry about Nicky, with a particularly heavy workload ahead of me. As a chef, I had to organise the catering for a huge charity event after a full day's teaching. The pains started during the frenzied preparations. I began to sweat profusely and finally had to give in and sit down. I didn't know it at the time, but I was having a massive heart attack. When the pain became unbearable, I phoned Andrew, who took me straight to hospital. I stayed there for three weeks, and afterwards retired from my job as lecturer. Andrew was a huge support to me throughout. I don't know what I would have done without him.

'I used to pester Andrew constantly to go over to Nicky's house to see if they were back from Libya, but he was adamant that I recuperate fully before confronting that situation. He made me wait for three months before driving over. This time the house was empty. Literally. It was obvious that no one was living there. I couldn't understand it. We drove to the salon, where I was informed that "Amal" was now living in the flat upstairs. Standing back, I looked up to the flat and could see Nicky at the window. She withdrew quickly when she saw me and disappeared from view. I stood at the door and rang and rang the bell, but she wouldn't answer. Eventually, she opened a window and leant out, screaming abuse at me. I looked up at her in horror, as her words rained down on me, not recognising this stranger as my quiet, loving daughter. She'd never sworn at me in her life. And now here she was, her face contorted in anger, yelling terrible words of hatred at me to go away and never come back. I didn't go. I stayed rooted to the spot, crying uncontrollably, at a loss to know what to say or do. She disappeared and for a fleeting moment, I hoped that she'd seen reason and was going to relent and let me in. Instead she returned with yet more screams, together with a boiling kettle, which she emptied out all over me.'

'My God, did she burn you?' I asked.

'No. As soon as I realised what she was doing, instinct or reflex kicked in,' said Margaret. 'I moved away. Only got a few drips on my head. It wasn't that bad. I just couldn't believe it was happening.'

She looked at her watch. 'I've been rattling on for ages,' she said. 'Time to make the coffee.'

She got up and went through to the hall, and brought back two silver framed photographs, which she handed to me. 'This is Nicky, and these are her children,' she said, disappearing into the kitchen.

I picked up the larger frame. A beautiful, petite, raven-haired beauty stared up at me, with deep-brown eyes and ruby-red lips. I don't know what I was expecting, but it wasn't this. Nicky was absolutely, stunningly beautiful. Her hair was thick and lustrous, reaching down to her waist, and her eyes crinkled cheekily, framed in a delicate, heart-shaped, smiling face.

I realised I had assumed she would be blonde, having seen Margaret with her fair hair and knowing all about the Arab man's penchant for a blonde trophy wife. In fact I had built up quite a strong image of Nicky in my mind's eye, from Margaret's story so far. I had pictured a frail, lined, anxious woman, looking older than her years, with straggly blonde hair, roughly tied back off her face. This girl staring up at me now was immaculately made up, confident and happy, and would have fitted in perfectly alongside any celebrity in a glossy magazine. Obviously this was a picture of a younger Nicky, before her trials with Karim.

I turned my attention to the smaller frame. Two children stood on a beach, smiling. Margaret's grandchildren,

Mahmoud and Latifa. They looked about seven and five.

As Margaret returned with coffee and sponge cake, I held the larger picture out in front of me and remarked, 'Nicky's beautiful, isn't she?'

The tears sprang uninvited into her eyes, as Margaret took the frames and returned them to the table in the hall. 'Yes, she was,' she replied quietly. 'It's the best picture she's ever had taken.'

I have a picture of myself at home, which sits in a large frame on a table in the hallway. It was taken by a school photographer when I was teaching in Cairo. I was unveiled and we went outside for the shots. He managed to get the light just right, so that the sun shone down on my blonde hair, making it look sleek and healthy, and he captured an air of confidence and calm in my expression. At the time, Leila, my first child, would have been a tiny baby; in fact I was breast-feeding, and had to leave the children in the classroom with a cleaner every time Leila needed a feed. It was at the beginning of my new life as a wife and mother, when I was trying so hard to do everything right. We had just moved into our own flat, and I was still besotted with Omar and optimistic about our future together. Although generally not photogenic, I look radiant in the picture; ironically, it's the best one I've ever had taken, before or since – just like Nicky.

We sat quietly for a few minutes, drinking coffee and nibbling the sponge cake. I sensed that it was taking a lot out of Margaret to speak so candidly, and I didn't want to rush her. I understood completely the extent to which Nicky had been obsessed with Karim, and I was aware that Margaret knew that now. I was convinced that when she reached the end of the story she would experience a huge sense of relief.

'I haven't many pictures of the children,' Margaret said. 'Like I said, we didn't see a lot of them. Karim seemed to dote on Mahmoud, but we found out years later that he was less than pleased when Latifa arrived.'

I nodded knowingly. 'He wanted another son.'

'That's right. He got over it eventually. After all, there's his other child from his first wife. That was a boy.'

I'd forgotten all about that. 'Does he see much of him?' I asked.

Margaret shook her head. 'Never had anything to do with him. The CSA had to chase him for maintenance and everything. He didn't want to pay out anything for his own son. I don't understand him at all.'

'So why did they move back into the flat above the salon?' I asked, impatient to hear more of the story.

'We found that out later,' said Margaret. 'I want to tell you how things happened, in order. At that time, all Andrew and I knew was that their family home was empty. We drove round to the three terraced properties, to find new owners living there. It was a mystery. One we had no idea how to solve.'

'So what did you do?'

'Well, the children both attended their local primary

school. We knew that Nicky walked there with them every morning, and picked them up in the afternoon. So I drove to the school to meet her and get her to tell me what was going on. At first, she wouldn't speak at all, just kissed the children and hurried off, ignoring my calls. But I persisted. Then she tried shouting at me to leave her alone, but I still turned up, every morning, pleading with her. Finally, one day, she stayed by the fence, watching her children go into school and let me stand beside her. I didn't say anything at all. I just stood there praying. Praying that this would be the day I'd get through to her. After a few minutes, she extended her hand slowly from beneath her coat and grasped mine. We stood there, like that, saying nothing, me shaking with sobs, until finally she began to talk. She told me that Karim had been gambling, and got himself into debt. He'd had to let all the houses go to pay it off. They were fine now, she said. And she squeezed my hand and was gone.'

Margaret looked at me and smiled. 'It wasn't much, but at that moment, I could have jumped for joy. My daughter had broken her silence and was talking to me again. I drove home full of renewed hope that things between us would improve.'

'How wonderful. Well done,' I said. 'What a bastard Karim is, though. Losing all that property. She'd worked all hours God sent to make a decent living for them all, and he gambled it all away. Surely by now she could see through him?'

'You'd certainly think so, wouldn't you?' Margaret

shrugged. 'On the contrary, however. After that day, I returned to speak to her again, but the old Nicky was back, ignoring me and shuffling away without a word. I was crushed. Overnight, I had lain in bed, too excited to sleep, pestering Andrew with my plans for the future and how it would involve Nicky and the children. I might just as well have been dreaming. It was cloud-cuckoo-land. I should have known.

'I went home confused and upset,' she continued. 'Andrew said we should leave things alone for a while before we tried again. After three weeks of silence, I was going mad with worry and drove once more to the school. There was no sign of Nicky or the children. Assuming one of them must be ill, I went to the flat and was surprised to see a big notice across the salon window. It had closed down. There was no answer at the flat. I could feel the first stirrings of panic in the base of my stomach. Where were they? Who could I ask? There was no one around. I had lost my daughter. Again.

'At home, I was inconsolable. Andrew tried everything, even getting angry and shouting. Then the accusations started. I was letting things get out of hand, neglecting the other three girls, never mind him, he said. Nicky was a big girl now and she'd made it crystal clear she didn't want us in their lives, he said. "Get over it," he said.

'Sounds like things were pretty desperate. He didn't know what to do, and he was panicking, that's all,' I said. 'My dad expected my mum to handle me emotionally, in the same

184

way. It's probably something to do with the mother–daughter bond that fathers assume exist. They leave that side of things to the women to deal with. When the going gets tough, they panic and make things worse by turning on their wives, to deflect attention from them. Instead of support, the mums get blame thrown at them. They feel hurt and wronged. And so the screaming and shouting begins. Classic.'

Margaret nodded. 'That's how it was exactly. But one good thing did come out of it all. In his anger, Andrew bellowed at me that if I was so damned worried, then why the hell didn't I visit the school and speak to the teachers to see what was going on. I don't know why I hadn't thought of it before. But suddenly, there it was, right in front of me. A glimmer of hope.

'I remember looking at Andrew, pacing up and down the rug in front of the gas fire and smiling through his ranting. I got up and held his bewildered face in both my hands, kissed him on the cheek and whispered, "Thank you", before driving once more to the little school. They were able to tell me that Mahmoud and Latifa had left and were now attending a school in a town thirty miles away. They'd sent their records on, they said.'

Without putting a name to this town, it is enough to know that this was a market town, back in the direction of where we were now sitting. About ten miles away, all told.

'I know I went to the school for information,' Margaret said, 'but I was expecting to hear that one of the children was ill, or something like that. This was nothing short of a bombshell. How had they all upped and left in such a short time? And, more importantly, why? I drove straight to the town, parking in the market square, and waited for the children to come out of school. As they did so, I stopped as many mums as I could and asked if they knew my grand-children, who were new to the area. After a desperate ten minutes of blank looks and shaking of heads, one little boy said he knew Latifa. I asked if they had any idea where they were living. His mum looked slightly embarrassed when she said she didn't know exactly, but I could try the tall building at the back of the square.

'I thanked her and walked in the direction of her nod until I reached what from the outside appeared to be some sort of warehouse. It towered up into the sky, above all the other buildings around it. There must have been five floors, with several large, dusty windows on the fascia of each floor. The huge, wooden front door was ajar.'

Margaret took another tissue and was crying as she spoke. 'It was like entering a different world. I stepped gingerly inside and stared in horror into the dark, cavernous space. It was literally filled with people, foreigners, refugees, I don't know. There were old bits of furniture scattered around, broken chairs, sagging settees, cupboards with the doors hanging off. Bags of clothes littered the floor; yet more clothes hung from crude washing-lines strung this way and that; a burning stove glowed red somewhere in the middle; and the noise was deafening. Women swathed in long clothes and veils sat about, while ragged children ran around aimlessly. From every corner came shouting; the children screamed as they played, the women shouted across to one another, each trying to overpower the noise of the children.'

My eyes widened as I listened. She was describing a scene I had often experienced before. Living with a large family in Cairo, we had often got together in one room, or gone to the zoo and sat on the grass, or even gone to Alexandria once and sat in a large garden together. The adults never attempted to discipline their children; it was expected that they would shout and scream and run about and chase each other. They were never asked to sit down and eat; rather they 'ate on the move'. So a mother would wrap some cheese in a piece of pitta bread, for instance, and try and get the child to take a bite in passing, or a spoonful of yoghurt. Wherever we were, with so many women and children together, the day predictably ended in chaos. And the noise was always deafening. I would sit on the outside and watch the girls play. They were the only two who actually sat down with me, ate their lunch all up, and went off to play again. Oh yes. I could almost feel the atmosphere in that warehouse, right there in Margaret's sitting-room.

The disturbing thing was, however, that this wasn't thousands of miles away, in Egypt. This was in the centre of a busy market town, not ten miles from where I had grown up. It was almost unbelievable that such a thing could go on under our noses without us having any idea. This was the 1990s, for God's sake. I shuddered involuntarily and tuned back in to Margaret, who had begun to speak again.

'No one challenged me as I picked my way across that vast space towards the large wooden staircase on the back wall. The first and second floors told similar stories; my heart broke as I peered into shadowy corners and crannies, looking for Nicky.'

Margaret suddenly buried her head into her tissue, trying to control herself. She spoke between sniffs, 'She was on the third floor. Filthy, huddled on a bare, stained mattress, with a huge belt around her waist. Both children were strapped to her and she was clinging onto them as if it was for dear life. When I approached, she shrank away, unwilling to talk at first. But eventually she told me that everything they had was gone – the business, the houses, the salon, the lot. Karim had got into difficulties with his gambling, she said, and there was nowhere else for them to go. When I tried to hug the children, she screamed. It was a howling, desperate scream, so loud that I put my hands in the air and backed away. I told her they could all come with me, but she shook her head vehemently and said that Karim was doing his best and would come for them shortly. She had no idea where he was. No matter how much I begged her to leave that hovel and come home with me, she blatantly refused. When I mentioned taking the children, she turned into a snarling, threatening stranger, as if devil-possessed. She clung to the belt tying them to her and said she would die before anyone ever took them from her. Eventually, I agreed to leave, but managed to get her to agree to move out if I could find decent accommodation for them.'

She blew her nose and threw the tissue into the bin. 'That was it,' she said. 'I was on a mission. I drove home as fast as I could and phoned the council. I kicked up such a stink; they gave me an interview that very afternoon and offered Nicky a council house in the same town where the salon had been. I couldn't believe our luck. I went back to visit them, taking food and a few other comforts, and this time, Nicky was calmer and more willing to talk. She seemed excited at having somewhere to go, even though it was a very run-down property, with boarded up windows and not even a proper floor. I felt sick having to leave them there again, but she would not budge, insistent that Karim would come to get them. He would be angry if he thought I'd found them in this state, you see, and would have taken it out on Nicky for embarrassing him. The fear in her eyes was plain enough to see, but it was useless to ask. I knew she would never admit that he was abusing her.

'The council said they'd paint the house and, true to their word, they had finished by the weekend, and even put a plastic covering on the floor in the main room. At the time, we didn't have a lot of money, but I scrabbled round, buying second-hand bits and borrowing others, until the house was fairly presentable. A week to the day that I had walked into that god-forsaken warehouse, I emerged for the last time with my daughter and grand-children, to take them to their new home. Nicky thought it was a palace. She was delighted and threw her arms around me and thanked me. I returned the hug and was again sharply reminded of her frailty. Nicky was no more than a bag of bones.

'The council had stipulated that they would house only Nicky and the children, and Karim must not live there. Nicky agreed to this and, for a couple of weeks, we had fun starting a new life. The children went back to their old school and Andrew and I drove over every day to help. When Nicky suggested she could manage by herself and asked me to just drop by at the weekend, I thought nothing of it. But when the weekend arrived, I could see that someone else had been living there. And I knew without asking who that someone else was. I stood in the living-room and faced Nicky with my suspicions. It was true. He was back. Where had he been? With another woman.'

'How do you know?' I asked.

'Nicky told me, and later, Karim himself didn't bother to deny it. He stayed overnight with his "girlfriend", came to see the children before they left for school and left at around five in the afternoon. He had no shame, that man. He wanted to marry this woman and take her to live in Libya with him. He even brought her to Nicky's house, taking her into the front room. Nicky was allowed only in the middle room and the kitchen, and would have to make tea for them or anything else they fancied. It was sickening.'

'But why did Nicky put up with it?'

'If she didn't, she'd lose Karim, and if she lost Karim, he'd take the children away from her. Those two little mites were the only things in the world she cared about. Often, she'd not bother sending them to school, if Karim was in a particularly bad mood, frightened that he might take them from there. I left that day, with Nicky saying she'd be in touch, knowing that she wouldn't be.'

'And was she?' I was bursting to know.

Margaret shook her head resignedly. 'After all we'd done to set her up and sort her out, he breezes in and it's all wiped out. We knew it wouldn't be long before the council found out he was living there, and then what would they do? As it turned out, I would have preferred a visit from the council to the one I got from the police any day,' she said.

'The police?'

'It was about three weeks later. The doorbell rang. A policeman and policewoman were standing on the doorstep. After establishing who I was, they came in and said I should sit down, as they had some bad news. Nicky had been subjected to a terrible, frenzied attack. She had under-gone massive surgery and was fighting for her life at that very moment in hospital. The policeman said she was not expected to live more than a few hours.'

As she spoke, Margaret's eyes glazed over; she was reliving this terrible time, moment by moment. 'Andrew drove. It seemed to take an age to get there, and all the time I was trying to come to terms with the fact that my little girl was dying. By the time we reached the hospital, I had almost convinced myself that it couldn't be Nicky, it had to be someone else. It couldn't be my little girl. But it was. My beautiful, intelligent, foolish daughter was lying amid a mass of tubes in intensive care in a coma. I couldn't bear it!'

With a sob, Margaret went on, 'She had been hacked from the base of her pubic bone right up to her breasts and then horizontally across her stomach, so that all her intestines and innards had fallen out when she dragged herself out of the house, screaming for help. A man had been working under his car at the house opposite and said she was surrounded by a sea of blood and was moaning every time she moved, until she finally collapsed. He had called the ambulance. Not only that, but her attacker had cut crosses over both nipples, and the doctors counted twenty-one stab wounds all over her body . . .'

Margaret put her hand to her mouth and sobbed. I rushed over to hold her and we rocked gently together, me feeling her raw grief.

'And where was Karim during all this?' I asked.

'Nowhere to be seen. We thought it was him. It had to be. The police sectioned the area off and treated it as a full-scale murder investigation. DNA results revealed that the only other adult in the house was that brute, Karim. He had disappeared again, of course.'

'And the children?'

'At school. The attack had taken place in the middle of the day. A police officer had gone to the school to wait with them until I was able to get there and take them home. Andrew stayed with them while I returned to the hospital. I sat, clinging on to Nicky's bony hand, talking to her constantly, begging her – no, ordering her – to fight, to hang on, to use every last bit of strength she had left to stay alive.'

I realised that while Margaret was talking, I was still kneeling at her feet, clasping her hands in mine. For some reason, I had assumed Nicky was still alive. The depth of Margaret's sadness was beginning to sink in. She had kept this inside her for all these years. And now it was spilling out of her like a waterfall. How on earth had she coped for so long? I looked at her with renewed admiration and respect. I gently released her hands and moved back to my place on the sofa.

'I'm sorry, Margaret,' I said, acutely aware of the ludicrous inadequacy of my words.

'It's all right,' she replied. 'I really needed to tell someone. But it couldn't be just anyone.' She looked up, imploring me, 'You understand, don't you?'

'Completely,' I said.

With a sigh, she continued. 'The police set about looking for Karim, as there was no evidence pointing to anyone else. Of course, they didn't find him. He obviously had his spies in the area, telling him he was wanted for murder, so we knew he'd never show his face. I sat with Nicky all through that day and all night.'

She looked up at me again and said, 'And do you know what? She didn't die that day. She hung on. Through the night and then the next day. The doctors were baffled, but my little girl clung on. She didn't die.'

She was quiet. I was stunned. We sat there in silence,

while I digested what she'd just said. 'So she's alive after all?' I whispered.

'She hung on until her conditioned stabilised. After three weeks she awoke from the coma. It was nothing short of a miracle,' sniffed Margaret. 'Andrew and I were run ragged, driving the grandchildren to their school thirty miles away and picking them up again, me sitting constantly with Nicky. We were ratty, stressed and constantly arguing over the slightest thing. Deep inside, we were not expecting Nicky to pull through, and the anxiety was getting to us. When she stabilised, and there was a glimmer of hope, we discovered a new-found energy, which pulled us through. It was marvellous really.

'The police visited Nicky to ask her about the attack as soon as she was able to talk. She rambled on about a stranger entering the house. She described him as a short, white man with very blond hair. The exact opposite, if there is one, of Karim. Andrew and I weren't fooled. She was protecting him. But why? No matter what we said, she refused to be drawn on the subject, adamant that the attack had nothing whatsoever to do with Karim.

'Eventually, she recovered enough to be brought home. The children were over the moon, and were very understanding, being extra careful not to jump on her or be boisterous, bringing her anything she needed. It was a happy time. The headmaster of the children's school drew me aside one day to say how delighted he had been with their recent attendance record. We knew they had had the odd day off, but were shocked to hear that Nicky usually used to come for them halfway through the afternoon, and sometimes they had had four days out of five off in a week. Mahmoud, at eight, had been struggling to read or write. Within a month, he was coming on in leaps and bounds, and was able to word-process confidently, using the spellcheck. It was a magical time. Which didn't last. Karim reappeared, as large as life, banging on the front door, crying and pleading to see his wife and children. What a performance.'

'Did you let him in?'

'We had to. He was upsetting the children and Nicky was begging us to see what he had to say. He waltzed in, kissing the children and swinging them around and then crying with Nicky as he innocently asked her what had happened. He'd been away on business, he said. He'd made a bit of money and they could all live together very shortly. I watched this monster dancing around my sitting-room, conning his way so easily back into my vulnerable daughter's life. And I wanted to kill him.'

'My God, Margaret! Where is the end to your suffering?' I cried, horrified.

'There is no end. I know that now. I just have to live with it. Like you. Anyway, while we got on with the day-to-day care of Nicky and the children, the police were showing interest in Karim. Although it was no longer a murder investigation, they brought him in for questioning with regard to attempted murder. But he got off.'

'He what?' I couldn't believe my ears.

She spoke in an expressionless voice. 'It was a till receipt that did it. From Morrisons. Forensics had put the time of the attack at between 12.50 and 1.00 p.m. The till receipt was dated and the time was 1.05.'

I was dumbfounded. 'But surely they didn't fall for that?' I said. 'That could have been anyone's receipt. That's no evidence of his whereabouts at all.'

'It was enough for the police to let him go,' she replied. 'They asked him to turn out his pockets and it was stuffed inside with other bits. They certainly believed it was his, or they wouldn't have let him go.'

It was unbelievable. When would their lives take a turn for the better? Lady Luck certainly had deserted this unfortunate family.

'Karim visited most days, always attentive and anxious for Nicky to get well. Gradually, she relaxed in his presence and began to smile again. He opened a pizza shop in town, and started mentioning Victim Support. He reckoned that Nicky was entitled to a lot of money if she put in a claim. At first, she laughed off the idea, but hastily changed her attitude when the old, domineering Karim reared his head. He eventually made an appointment with a solicitor for her, and started the ball rolling. Nicky became anxious and nervous again; we guessed Karim must be venting his anger on her and bullying her while we were at work although, true to form, Nicky vehemently denied it. As the weeks rolled by, I decided to take the bull by the horns and ask Karim what his plans were exactly. He was entering our house every day, eating our food, providing his family with nothing as usual. I wanted to face him alone so, one evening, I drove to his pizza place. The front of the shop was deserted, so I wandered through to the back, and froze on the spot. There was Karim, lying on a table on top of a girl, with his hand firmly under her bra. They were kissing passionately. It was more than I could take. I cleared my throat and calmly told him I would return when he was less busy. Then I left.'

'How on earth did you hold your temper?' I asked, incredulous. 'I would have exploded'

'Andrew and I guessed as much,' she said flatly. 'Let's face it, gambling, casinos, women all fit in with the lifestyle he's been living. And getting away with,' she added bitterly. 'That night just confirmed our suspicions. He ran after me in the street and said he was doing nothing wrong. "I don't think Nicky will see it like that," I remember telling him. But he just laughed in my face. Do you know what he said then?' she asked me. 'I'll never forget those words. He said, "Amal believes what I tell her to believe. If you cross me, you will lose her." And he turned and walked back into the shop, leaving me standing there helplessly. He was right and we both knew it.

'The next week, we arrived home after work to an empty house. There was a note on the kitchen table, telling me that they had gone to live in Libya. No forwarding address, no phone number. They hadn't even said goodbye. For the umpteenth time, I had lost my daughter. I was distraught. Nothing anyone could say consoled me and I almost had a breakdown. Andrew and I were under great strain. He's such a strong character, so determined that he was not going to let me suffer, but I was as low as I have ever been. Night after night, I would sit with a pile of photos, poring over and over them and crying to myself. I felt so alone. Nobody understood me. My three daughters took me in hand, showering me with love and attention and leaving our other grandchildren with us, until I was finally able to pull myself together. I don't know how I managed it. I began making efforts to respond to Andrew, and concentrated on getting through a day at a time.'

My mother flashed before my eyes as she said this. After we had escaped from Egypt, she had tried to describe how she'd coped while I was away. We hardly ever spoke on the phone, as we didn't have one and I was embarrassed to ask Omar's father to use his phone when I couldn't pay for the call. Instead we relied on letters. Mum said she'd become so depressed and generally preoccupied that she and Dad went through a shaky patch over it. She didn't know when she would see me again and it was tearing her apart, she said. In the end, she'd coped by taking one day at a time. Like Margaret.

'So when did you see her again?' I asked.

'We heard nothing for four years,' she answered. 'It had been so long that I despaired of ever seeing her again. I used to lie in bed, thinking, "What if one of us were to have a serious accident, or die? She'd never know. How would she feel if she ever found out?" It was such a worry. But we didn't have a clue as to their whereabouts. Gradually, with the passing of time, our initial hopes faded into resignation that she was lost forever.

'It was a Wednesday,' she continued. 'Out of the blue, Karim called and said Amal was coming home to get the Victim Support money. She would be flying into Heathrow from Tripoli at 6 p.m. the following evening. Then he hung up. No explanations, no apology for leaving without a word. We didn't have a chance to respond. Andrew was left open-mouthed, holding the receiver.

'We rushed around, getting time off work, organising what we could before driving to Heathrow. It was almost surreal; we spoke little on the way down, in a kind of daze. With no flight details, we were dismayed to find that there were no direct flights into Heathrow from Tripoli that evening. There was one flight, however, that had gone from Tripoli to Germany and then on to Heathrow. We plumped for that one and eagerly waited at the barrier. The passengers took around twenty minutes to come through. Nicky was not one of them. Desperate, I rushed to the desk for information, but was not allowed access to the passenger list. We sat and ordered coffee to calm our nerves and decide on what on earth to do next. I was just draining my cup, when I looked over and saw her.

'A solitary figure, holding a cotton bag with a few clothes trailing from it, was moving very slowly towards us. I nudged Andrew and said it was Nicky, but he said it wasn't. I rushed up to her anyway, calling, "Nicky". There wasn't a flicker of recognition in her face, and for a moment I had doubts that it was her. But then I shouted, "Amal", and she turned towards me. It *was* her. In an instant, Andrew was at her side, scooping her into his arms and carrying her to the car. She weighed four and a half stone.'

I gasped. 'You were so lucky to have found her,' I said. 'So many things could have gone wrong.'

'Don't I know it?' said Margaret. 'We took her to a motorway café, but she was unable to do more than sip at a glass of water. Her bag was full of rags, so filthy I wouldn't use them to wash the kitchen floor. We set about caring for her and making her well again.'

I was relieved. 'At last you had your daughter back, and this time for good,' I remarked. 'But what about the children?'

'She was expecting them to follow her very soon. Apparently, she had only agreed to come back if Karim promised to bring the children. He was waiting for their visas, she said. Gradually, I nursed her back to health – physical health, that is. Mentally, Nicky was very ill. She was no longer the daughter I knew. The doctor prescribed four lots of strong medication, which did manage to stabilise her somewhat, but she had lost her mind.

'She would often curl up in a chair in the foetal position, like a lost puppy, holding a cushion and rocking back and forth, eyes staring this way and that nervously. Or she'd suddenly turn, screaming and shouting, her eyes wild. If we tried going out for a quiet walk and met some innocent person coming in the opposite direction, she would hiss, 'Fatwa, fatwa,' at them over and again, convinced they'd been sent from Libya to kill her. Television aerials bothered her immensely; she said spies had set them up as radar links to Libya to come and kill her. The nights were the worst; she would rant and rave in her troubled sleep, screaming out desperate pleas for Karim to stop. "Please don't hurt me again," she would whimper, or "Don't let them rape me again today. No more today." '

The tears were now flowing freely down Margaret's cheeks; she spoke through them, making no effort to wipe them away. 'If taking my precious daughter away from us wasn't enough, it was becoming clear that she had suffered abuse of the most monstrous, inhumane kind, and at the will of her husband, Karim. At first, she wouldn't talk about her time out there, but as the weeks rolled by and the medication took a stronger hold, she broke her silence little by little.

'Karim's family were very poor and lived on some sort of farm. They had flown to Tripoli Airport and taken a taxi for a little while, but Karim paid the driver off and made them all get out, saying they would walk the rest of the way. They ended up walking for four whole days. She had absolutely no idea where the farm was. She spent every day of the next four years on that farm, not leaving even for shopping, or to take the children to school. Karim beat her for the slightest thing and treated her with contempt, bringing friends in to rape her while he watched. After a year, he took another wife and moved her into the farmhouse. Nicky became surplus to requirements.'

Margaret was sobbing now, taking large gulps and talking all the while, determined to get the whole story out. The atmosphere in the room was heavy with emotion; I was crying quietly into my hankie.

'Nicky was . . . dumped . . . in a dog kennel outside. They . . . tied her up like a dog. The only food she ate . . . was the scraps . . . that Mahmoud and Latifa threw her. She lived . . . like . . . that for three long years. If Karim wanted to watch one of his friends raping her, she would be hauled out and under a cold shower, and thrown on a mattress inside the house. Afterwards, she was ordered back to her kennel. She would have died in there if Karim hadn't seen another opportunity to get his filthy hands on some money. Suddenly she became useful to him again.'

'The Victim Support money,' I said, remembering Karim's phone call. 'But did he honestly believe that if he let her go, she would ever come back to him?'

Margaret blew her nose, nodding in agreement, and took a few deep breaths. 'This is quite therapeutic,' she said. 'But also very traumatic for me.'

'I never spoke about my time in Egypt when we first escaped,' I said. 'I preferred to pretend it had happened to someone else. I told my parents enough to satisfy their concerns, but then I buried it. Funnily enough, as they grew up, neither Leila nor Amira asked me any awkward questions about their real father. I know Leila put Amira in the picture at some stage, but it made it all the easier to put it behind me and move on. Only my mother dying of cancer could persuade me to dig out those memories and write my story down. It completely overwhelmed me how, once I'd opened that door just an inch, the whole nasty experience came rushing into my consciousness like a tidal wave. It was as if I was still there, experiencing all the smells and the heat. Like it was only yesterday.' I shuddered at the memory. 'I'm glad I wrote the book now,' I went on. 'I don't have to carry it all around inside. It's almost like being set free.'

'Nicky was home and that was great,' said Margaret, returning to the story. 'But she fretted continually about the children. "Karim promised to bring them," she kept saying. "He promised to telephone every week at three o'clock, on a Friday." It must have been about three months after her arrival that they made the first call. She was deliriously happy to hear their voices. Papa was still trying to get the visas, they said. They would see her soon, they said. Nicky smothered the telephone with kisses and cradled it against her cheek. Then Karim came on the line and immediately asked about the money. She had been in no state to do anything yet and it was not what he wanted to hear. When he rang off, she sat huddled in a corner of the hall for about an hour, rocking and muttering to herself.'

'He still had control, even over the phone,' I mused. 'That must have hindered her progress, mustn't it?'

'More than that,' said Margaret. 'She now pestered me to go back to the solicitor and see what had happened to her claim. I didn't think there was any point, but she wouldn't rest until I agreed. As it turned out, she had been awarded several thousand pounds, but she had not claimed it within the time limit of two years, rendering it null and void. This news sent Nicky into a frenzy. She needed that money, she said. Without the money, Karim would never let her see her children again.

'Finally, to calm her down more than anything else, I wrote a heartfelt letter, explaining that no one had told us that our application had been successful, and we therefore didn't know Nicky had been awarded any money. I outlined the attack she had endured and pleaded for a sympathetic ear, for someone to understand and consider reopening the case. It must have tugged at the heartstrings of whoever read it, because it worked. The case was reopened.'

'That's your first bit of luck so far,' I said.

'We had to go through numerous sessions with the solicitor, and have recent photographs of Nicky's scars taken,' said Margaret. 'Even after five years, the scarring was horrific. Her body was a mutilated mass of twisted, droopy skin and pitted with scars. She refused to reveal her whole body for the photos, keeping her underwear on, but the evidence was still as clear as ever. When the case was compiled, we were told it would take approximately two years to come to court.

'It was another couple of months before Karim phoned again. When he heard the news, he slammed down the phone in anger. It was another year before he made further contact.'

'And the children?' I asked. 'Did they get their visas?'

'They were never going to come,' Margaret said matter-of-factly. 'We got on with living. Progress was slow but steady and, after a year, Nicky was doing well, able to cope with familiar situations without having a screaming fit. There was always a sadness in her eyes, and I wasn't able to reach her emotionally any more. I had to treat her as if she were a child again. But we muddled along. Then *he* called.'

'Karim?'

Margaret nodded. 'He managed to persuade Nicky that she could live on her own now and should look for a flat. Then he would send her the children, he said. He didn't want them living with us. Nicky was their mother and she should have her own place for them. Nicky came off the phone like a woman possessed. She had to find a flat, she said. That very day. Then the children would come. Once again, our pleas fell on deaf ears. We ended up finding her a flat about five miles away. Once again, we rallied round with bits of furniture, curtains, bits and bobs to make it homely and she moved in. Still unable to go out without us, she was still reliant on us for shopping trips, but otherwise, she kept the flat as neat as a new pin, ready for when the children came.

'Another year passed. Every Friday, without fail, Andrew drove over to collect Nicky, who waited by the phone. She received one call, another hollow promise, giving her false hope that she would see her babies again. Then, out of the blue, I received a call, instructing me that Nicky's hearing would be that week. It was to be held in a city two hours' drive away. We arranged to travel up with the solicitor. Andrew said he would pick him up on the way.

'On the morning of the hearing, luck deserted us. The solicitor informed us that he was unable to attend. He said it wouldn't be a problem; would I act for Nicky? All I had to do was read through the case notes; it would only be a little hearing and over in ten minutes or so. We could pick up the case notes on our way through.'

Margaret shook her head. 'I was bewildered,' she said. 'I didn't know the first thing about court proceedings. All I did know was that we had waited two years for this hearing, and if I didn't do this, Nicky would lose her entitlement for a second time. Hobson's choice. I didn't want to let her down. But if I acted for her, would I let her down anyway?

'The solicitor said I could do it with my hands tied behind my back, so I agreed. We picked up the case notes, which I read on the journey. There were only a handful of sheets, so it didn't seem as daunting as I'd imagined. On our arrival, however, we were met by frowns of disapproval. Where was our solicitor? This was all highly irregular. And so on. We discovered that it was to be a full-blown hearing with a full court, not at all what our solicitor had led us to expect. We sat in a side room at a large table, while the situation was discussed. In the end, after questions and deliberations, it was agreed that under the circumstances I would be allowed to act for Nicky.

'The case notes were the next problem. "Is this *all?*" I was asked. When I nodded, there was another flurry as heads were once again put together. A woman entered, carrying two bulging files, which she set down heavily on the table in front of me. "The judge has put the hearing back, in order for you to read through the full complement of case notes," a woman informed me. "You have thirty minutes." She looked at Andrew. "I suggest you start with one file and you start with another, madam, or you'll never get through it all." There was no time to think. In a panic, Andrew and I sat intently and studied the contents of the files. As I read, my heart flipped over. The bulk of all the notes were hospital records. Nicky's records. Cracked ribs, broken jaw, broken wrists, dislocated shoulders, burns, bite marks – the list went on and on. I looked at the dates and gasped. She had suffered at the hands of that brute from the moment they met. The records started when she was eighteen. She had suffered so much, even when she was working hard to build up the business, before they were married. But there was no time to dwell on my discovery; I had an important duty in front of me.

'The court was so formal,' she went on. 'I'd never been in a courtroom before. Nicky was composed and calm, dressed demurely in a long, flowery dress. They questioned her for one and a half hours. She answered quietly and without fuss, a pathetic creature, out of place in this den of wolves. Then it was my turn. I was so nervous, I can't remember any specific details, but two hours later, they had finished with me. The judge made an award to Nicky of £20,000. He made the proviso, however, that the money was intended specifically for Nicky to build a new life, and not to be given away. Due to her mental state and the medication she relied on, he decided she would need help and support in using the money wisely. He therefore decreed that the cheque be made out to Andrew and me. He suggested that we withdraw £5,000 initially, for her to set up a hairdressing business, and then give her a monthly salary to live on. We all readily agreed to this. The ordeal was over.'

'Well done,' I said. 'You made the right choice. Two hours of stress is fair exchange for £20,000.'

'It depends how you look at it,' said Margaret.

'What do you mean?' I asked.

'At first, we were delighted,' she said. 'What a result. Nicky agreed with the conditions, and we honestly believed she'd finally got Karim out of her head. Then, a week later, the cheque arrived. Not made out to us, as the judge had ordered, but made out instead to Nicky. So much for an important court hearing.'

'At the end of the day, did that really matter?' I asked. 'You could still do the same with the money, no matter whose account it went into.'

'Well, we hoped so, but when I saw the cheque, my heart sank. Somehow, I knew it would change things in Nicky's mind, if she thought she had control of all that money. Unfortunately, I was right.'

'Oh, no,' I said. 'What did she do?'

'I decided to visit her and have a chat, before giving her

the cheque,' Margaret answered. 'Maybe I could persuade her to let me send it back and have it altered. But it was too late. I knew as soon as she answered the door. Somehow, she had been in touch with Karim. I could tell. She was nervous, on edge and in a very bad mood when she let me in. As soon as I mentioned the cheque, she demanded to know where it was. When I admitted I'd left it at home, she had a fit, screaming and shouting that I was a cow and she hated me and she needed that cheque now. I agreed to fetch it and she calmed down. Suddenly the anger had gone and she offered to make coffee. I relaxed and sat down.'

Margaret cleared her throat and continued. 'She approached me from behind and offered me the coffee. As I leaned over to take it from her, her arm was suddenly around my neck, her hand grabbing a fistful of hair, yanking my head upwards. Her eyes were wild and I felt a cold sensation on my neck. I realised in horror that it was a kitchen knife. She pressed the blade into my neck, and told me to get that cheque or she would kill me. At that moment, looking into her eyes, I could see only too well that she meant it. I could only nod weakly and whisper that I would go right away and bring it. Then she released me.

'I drove home in turmoil, desperately worried for Nicky. How had she spoken to Karim? What had he convinced her to do now, with his lies? I returned with the cheque to find her standing behind her front door, snarling like a dog, knife in hand. "Give me the cheque, bitch, or I'll kill you," she spat. "Why are you doing this to yourself, darling?" I whispered, crying as I held out the cheque. She said nothing, grabbed the cheque and slammed the door in my face. That was the last time I ever saw her.'

I sat up in surprise. 'You mean, you never saw her again?'

'It was so unexpected,' Margaret went on. 'I knew she couldn't go out alone, so we did what we usually did when she had one of her "dos". We left her for a couple of days to calm down. These mood swings were very common, you know. Part of all of our lives. Anything could trigger her off, although she was always bad after contact with Karim. We'd got into the habit of leaving her until it passed. She would be meek and mild then, as if the "other" Nicky didn't exist. But this time, she did go out. With Terry.'

'Terry?'

'The man in the flat below. He became a very good friend to Nicky. Apparently, he used to hear her crying out in her sleep and went to see how he could help. He was gentle and kind, just the opposite of Karim and excellent therapy for Nicky. He grew very fond of her. We found out later that he'd gone with her to the bank.

'On the third day after our quarrel, we decided to do our supermarket shopping, get some supplies in for Nicky and use that as an excuse to go round and check on her. We returned home first, to unload our shopping, to find a letter had been hand-delivered, with a post-it note stuck on the top. It read, "Nicky wants me to tell you that I am taking her to the airport now to put her on a flight to Tripoli." It was signed, "Terry".'

Margaret was silent. Eager to know more, I pressed her to go on. 'You followed her, right?'

'Wrong. We telephoned the airport. The flight had already left. We spoke to Terry afterwards, who said his mate had delivered the note long after they'd left. Nicky wanted to be sure we wouldn't be able to stop her. Nicky had chosen hell over us. How do you think that made us feel?'

'I honestly can't imagine,' I whispered.

'Once again, she'd gone. We had no idea where, and no means of looking. We were helpless, condemned to sit and wait. It was a year later, just last year, as it happens, on Mother's Day, that the phone rang. I was the unfortunate person who answered it. Karim's voice boomed out, loud and clear. His wife, Amal, had died the previous day of a massive heart attack, he stated. I screamed at his words and collapsed, sobbing. Andrew rushed to the phone and begged Karim to give us half an hour to compose ourselves and would he please, please phone back, if he had any conscience at all? Karim agreed, and Andrew must have struck a chord with him somewhere because, on this so very important occasion, he did ring back. I was sane enough by then to demand that her body be sent home. Not possible, I was told. She had already been cremated. He was very sorry for us, he said. Andrew, with a flash of inspiration, asked him for a contact number. Goodbye, said Karim, and hung up. We've never heard from him since.'

I sat stock-still, horrified to hear the events unfold. After everything, all her trials and tribulations, she had gone back to her children and to her death. All this time Margaret had been sitting here, telling me her story, I was willing the ending to be a happy one, for Nicky to get well and be reunited with her children. That's for fairy tales, I realised. The reality is pure tragedy.

'How did you cope?' I asked.

'I don't think we did, really,' said Margaret candidly. 'We went to see our MP and spoke to the Foreign Office, but the advice was always the same: don't go to Libya, you'll never come back alive. As it was, we had nothing to go on, so it would have been like looking for a needle in a haystack. It was all a bit too much for me. One of my daughters said she would stay on the case and keep in touch with the authorities.

'When we were at the hearing, we had taken the files into the courtroom with us, and no one had actually requested that we return them. So I brought them home with us. After Nicky's death, I would get them out every day and sit, poring over every little detail, crying for her, reliving her pain. This went on for months. And the memories. They were all over the house, oozing form every corner. I was going mad with grief. I couldn't even be sure that Karim was telling the truth. What if he had been lying? What if Nicky was still alive? What was I to believe?

'Andrew's health had also taken a turn for the worse and he underwent a quadruple heart bypass. The house and garden was becoming too much for him. We finally put the house up for sale, but not before he sat me down and we had a heart-to-heart. It was time to move on, he said. Nicky would always have a special place in our hearts, and now we had to move on. So we did.'

She swung her arm out around the room. 'We moved here, last September, six months after Nicky died. The day before we moved, Andrew sat me down and put the files on my knee. I nodded and, as we had agreed, he watched as I shredded every last page. I had closed the final chapter on her pain and would try and look forward to remembering her in happier times. And then there's this.'

She opened her handbag and handed me a brown envelope. 'I carry it around with me all the time,' she said. 'Even if I change my handbag, I transfer it, and that's not like me. It's as if I still can't believe she's really dead. At last, I have some sort of closure.'

Carefully, I drew the single sheet of white paper from the envelope. It was from the Libyan authorities, addressed to the Foreign Office, certifying that Amal had died in Libya on 18 March 2004, aged 45. I read and reread the words, simply written, on unheaded notepaper.

'My daughter kept phoning the authorities and at last she has come up with a result,' said Margaret quietly. 'Do you know what day she received it?'

As I shook my head, she whispered, 'Mother's Day.'

She got up to look out at the garden. 'Come and look,' she gestured for me to join her. As I did so, she pointed down to a beautiful, sunlit spot of lawn. 'We have com-missioned a statue,' she said. 'It's Andrew's Easter present to me. A statue of Nicky. It's going to stand there. We're going to call it "Shy Girl".'

There was a lump in my throat as I left. We hugged tightly, and I promised to visit again, after Easter. A few days later, I was standing in the queue at the Post Office, when I noticed Margaret standing a little way in front.

'Hello, Margaret. How are you?' I smiled.

She smiled warmly in return. 'I'm fine, thanks,' she replied. 'My daughter and grandchildren are staying for Easter, but I'll be in touch after that.'

And we parted. To all outward appearances, we were just a regular mum and a regular grandmother, who had regular, uneventful lives. Invisible women.

16

Shannon

Shannon contacted me via my website, using the support section, which enables people to speak to me privately. And she frightened me half to death with her letter.

'Dear Susannah,' she had written. 'How safe is this site? I really need to talk to you. I'm trying to be brave and go ahead with it but, like you, I've chickened out every time so far. Everything is ready this time. If only I could be sure . . . I will wait a day for your reply. With love, Rosie.'

Fumbling for the right keys, I logged on to my secure website in order to reply. 'Hi, Rosie, you're as safe as houses. Fire away, love, Jacky,' I typed as fast as I could, my fingers flying over the keyboard, and slammed down the send button.

As soon as I'd clapped eyes on the letter, I knew she was serious. She was contemplating suicide. Those few sentences described my emotions exactly when I was in a similar state in Egypt. I used to prepare everything, but at the end of the day, it was myself who wasn't ready, who wasn't brave enough to take that final leap. I used to whisper to myself, 'If only I could be sure . . .'

I drummed my fingers nervously on the desk as I waited. 'Please be on time, please be on time,' I whispered.

The trouble was, it was more than a day after she'd written to me. The email had come through on Saturday. I take the weekends off and only log in to the website on weekdays. It was now Monday morning.

After ten minutes there was no reply, so I left the site on the screen and got on with the day, checking for mail every half-hour or so. There was nothing more I could do. When there was still no message by eleven o'clock that evening, I had to assume that she had either given up on me or, worse, on herself. Sighing, hoping it was the former, I went to bed.

The next day, Tuesday, was a busy day for me. I got up at six and swam thirty lengths at the local pool, before putting in a day of supply teaching. It's funny how tired you feel when you work odd days, rather than flat out full time. I arrived home exhausted, trying to think of a good excuse why not to walk the dog, a good reason why fish and chips were good for you and an even better one why I should have the bathroom first.

Idly checking my mail, I saw, with delight, that Rosie had replied.

'It's okay,' I announced to my puzzled family. 'You have the bathroom, and forget the fish and chips. I'll make sweet and sour chicken, and walk Henry later. Just give me half an hour. Dinner at six-thirty.'

'Dear Jacky,' she began. 'Thank you so much for replying to my email. Now you have reassured me, I feel I can be open with you. I was so scared before that other people could access the site.

'I called you Susannah just in case. I feel safe enough to call you Jacky now,' she continued. 'My real name is Shannon. I'm twenty-eight years old. I'm Irish, and I live in Celbridge, just outside Dublin. Things have been bad for ages – years in fact. I've kept quiet, told no one, and things would have stayed that way if I hadn't have read your book, *Fatwa*. You went through so much and, like me, told no one. I'm interested to know how your life has turned out and how you managed to move on. Please find the time to reply. Love, Shannon.'

Later that evening, all chores completed, I settled down to reply.

'Hi there,' I wrote. 'You gave me a bit of a fright back there. By the time I read your letter, I feared you might have done something silly. Sounds like you've reached rock bottom.

'Anyway, at least we're talking now,' I went on. 'When I was in Egypt, there was no one I could talk to. It just wasn't worth the risk. An innocent comment, a careless remark could have got me into even more trouble than I was already in. The less anyone knew, the safer I was. Later, after our escape, it was even more important to keep things under wraps, because my husband, Omar, was looking for us. We had to appear as normal as the next person, so we tried to blend in and not speak about our past. But – and it's a hell of a big but – I had my parents to support us. Without their love, understanding and unending patience, I wouldn't be sitting here writing to you. It was slow, moving on, but the children helped. As time passed, I made a few good friends, in whom I confided, and to this day, they alone know the full story. They are my salvation. They helped me trust again. With my parents, the children and my husband, Ben, they pulled me up from the depths of depression.

'I suppose what I am trying to say,' I went on, 'is that I moved on when I found the courage to confide in people who didn't betray me. It started with Mum and Dad, but I never told them everything. They would never have been able to bear it. It was my mum who suggested I write it all down, and that was how I came to write *Fatwa*. That, in itself, was very therapeutic for me. Both my parents have died now, and I don't regret not telling them the worst bits. My friends had that pleasure, and they've been wonderful about it. Keeping stumm stops you from ever moving on. It means you don't trust anyone around you, and you're not strong enough to get out of the mess by yourself. Hope this helps. Love, Jacky.'

Shannon replied the following day. 'Dear Jacky, It's great talking to you. For the first time, I feel that I can talk to someone who would understand. I'm in a black hole at the moment, so low in spirit that I dread waking up in the mornings. I can't see how things will ever improve, and I can't carry on any longer as things stand. I couldn't possibly tell anyone around here; it would destroy the family and I can't be sure they would believe me anyway. So, if it's okay with you, I'd like to tell you everything. From the beginning. Love, Shannon.'

I decided that MSN would be the best way to communicate. That way, I could interrupt if I wanted to. Plus, Shannon would feel closer to me, as if we were having a normal, two-way conversation. Between us, we set aside a specific time to log on and talk to each other, twice a week.

The first time we talked, Shannon was anxious to spill everything out from the beginning. She started to type and the words fell out of her as she described her early childhood:

'I was six years old when Pappy shattered my world. We lived in a small, terraced house, Mammy, Pappy, my sis Maureen, three brothers and me. Pappy was a mechanic. Mammy worked evenings down the pub. She made sure Maureen and I were always in bed before she left, so we didn't miss her. Sean, Finn and Fergus were twelve, ten and seven. Maureen was the babby, only two years old. I slept with her in the tiny boxroom at the back of the house. Pappy was supposed to look after us, but he drank so much he fell asleep, or he went out drinking and left us alone in the house. He changed when the drink was inside him. Many times, I can remember waking up in the middle of the night, hearing him shouting and swearing at Mammy. He made her cry. I would push my face into the pillow so I couldn't hear. In the morning I would see the bruises on her face or arms, but she said nothing about it to me, and Pappy went off to work as usual, as if nothing at all had gone on.

'He would lash out at the boys, too, if they annoyed him.

He used a thick leather belt, which hung from a hook in the kitchen. He would take them into the yard and give them a thrashing. They were all terrified of that belt, especially Finn. Finn was the daredevil of the three, but he paid dearly for it. Pappy never raised his hand to Maureen or me, though. Only the boys. Mammy handled us.

'That fateful night, Pappy came into our bedroom and shook me gently awake.

' "Wake up, princess," he whispered. I can still smell the stench of his beer breath on my face, as he leant over and nuzzled my neck. I sat up in surprise and rubbed my eyes. Was it morning already? But the sky outside was still dark.

' "Where's Mammy?" I started to ask, but he clamped his filthy hand firmly over my mouth. "Ssh, we don't want to wake the babby, princess. Mammy's at the pub. I've come for a cuddle." And he made me shuffle up so that he could squash himself into the bed with me. He stroked my face over and again. "You're my special princess," he crooned. "I've come to make you feel good, to show you how much Pappy loves you." His hand moved to my cotton nightie and he began caressing my leg until the flimsy material rode up my thigh and I could feel the roughness of his palm against my skin. I didn't understand why he was doing this, but he was smiling all the time and in such a good mood. It seemed to make him happy, like the Pappy I loved, who didn't drink. Then he lurched forward and pressed his lips on mine.

' "Pappy, no," I cried, but he forced my lips apart with his own and thrust his tongue deep inside my mouth. I couldn't breathe. Then, suddenly, it was over and he pulled away. I lay there panting, when I felt his finger rubbing at me between my legs, gentle and then harder. By now I was terrified he was going to really hurt me, so I just lay there whimpering. He began to groan and then rolled off the bed and left the room. I hid under the sheet, spitting onto the pillow, trying to rid my mouth of the taste of my Pappy's breath. Two minutes later, he was back. He sat on the bed, lifted up the sheet to look at me and took my hands in his.

' "This must be our secret, princess," he said smiling. "It's what people do when they love each other more than anyone else. Mammy would cry if she knew I loved you more. So you must never tell Mammy what we do." He took me by the shoulders and looked me straight in the eyes. "Never," he repeated. I stared back at him silently and nodded, until he smiled again, gave me a quick hug, and was gone.

'This went on every couple of weeks, for four years. I told no one. By then, I knew it was wrong, and I felt dirty and ashamed. Far too frightened to refuse Pappy, I lay back each time with my eyes squeezed tightly shut, until he had finished. I didn't know how to stop him. And I had no idea how to tell Mammy. She cried a lot as it was. If I told her, she would be even more unhappy and it would all be my fault.

'I changed from a mischievous, chatterbox into a nervous, withdrawn, sly little girl. I developed strange habits, thinking that everyone was secretly talking about me and laughing at me behind my back. I used to creep out of my bedroom, squat on the landing and listen to conversations filtering up from downstairs, even though I didn't understand what they were all about. I lost my appetite at meal times, and started stealing bits of food from the cupboard to eat in my room where no one could see me.

'It happened suddenly. When I was ten years old, Pappy never came to my bed any more. Instead of going up to bed at seven o'clock with Maureen, I was allowed to stay downstairs until ten with my brothers. At first, I expected Pappy to find another place to take me to. I couldn't believe he would just stop. But he did. Little by little, the realisation that he was not going to touch me again started to sink in, as I watched him during the following weeks drink himself silly in front of the telly and fall asleep, or go off to the pub and come back with Mammy. I couldn't believe my luck. Lying in bed one night, I heard Mammy and Pappy coming up to bed. A few minutes later, Pappy came back out of his room and I froze in terror, staring through the darkness at my door handle, waiting for it to move slowly downwards, as he tiptoed in to see me. The handle didn't move; Pappy went down to the toilet and back to his room, coughing and slamming the door loudly behind him. Ripples of joy coursed through me and I smiled widely into the darkness. He was never coming to me again. The nightmare was over. Looking across at Maureen, asleep with her thumb in her mouth, I realised it must be because she was getting older. We slept together in an old double bed. Pappy was always very careful to be quiet, but now, at six years old, she would wonder what was going on if ever she woke up. That must be it, I decided. It's because of Maureen. I remember turning over in that big, lumpy bed and wrapping my arms around Maureen, who shrugged me off moodily. I didn't care; I hugged the pillow tightly instead and fell into a deep, uninterrupted sleep.

'Wow, I did it. I've told someone. That's a great feeling, you know.'

So engrossed in her story, I'd forgotten she was talking to me. She'd told it with such passion, I could imagine every terrifying scene, as if I was in that house with her.

'You've been through hell, haven't you?' I replied. 'I could feel your pain as you were telling me. Four years, Shannon. Thank God he stopped. It must have made a huge difference to your life.'

'It was amazing. I'd always been in trouble at school, running off and backchatting the teachers. They despaired over me. I didn't care. Mammy couldn't understand why I was so rude to people; mostly, if we had visitors, I'd ignore them and go up to my room. They made me feel dizzy. I didn't have any friends and couldn't read or write properly. Then, a year after everything stopped, I went to secondary school. It was brilliant. The first day, Mammy had to drag me to the door. But the old feelings – fear, nausea, fainting – didn't wash over me. Instead, the place looked busy and exciting. I felt stirrings of curiosity inside me, as if I wanted to go through that door and take part. I met new people who didn't frighten me. I made friends. The teachers were kind, and I was put into a special class for literacy, where they didn't make you feel stupid if you couldn't read. I wanted to try my best and I began to do better. I actually changed so much that I enjoyed school.'

'It's a shame these computers don't do hugs,' I wrote. 'I love happy endings.'

'Hold your horses, Jacky. This is only the beginning.'

'I know,' I replied. 'It's just that, when you began, you sounded pretty desperate. I assumed that your story would be, sorry to say it, full of hurt and sadness. It's wonderful to hear that you found happiness at school and could shake off those terrible experiences.'

'When you're a little girl, the world revolves around you,' Shannon continued. 'I was confused, upset and terrified when it was happening to me. I didn't know who I was any more. When it stopped, I was slowly able to be me again. I didn't give a thought to anyone else around me. As far as I was concerned, it was over. I was so blind.'

'You can't blame yourself. You've been through so much. It's only natural to think of yourself, just to survive. You were only ten years old, for God's sake,' I said. 'And you pulled yourself through. You need to pat yourself on the back, not beat yourself up.'

'Was it your mum?' I added, thinking on my feet. 'Did your dad become more abusive towards her after he stopped interfering with you?'

'Not really,' came the reply. 'Mammy loved Pappy to bits when he was sober. He was a nice Pappy then and they would laugh and joke with all of us. If any of us faced up to him when he was in drink, she would beg us to go to our rooms, not that Maureen or I ever tried it. Finn sometimes threw himself on Pappy's back, but he always finished up bruised and bleeding, and in the end it was worse for Mammy. She would never talk about it, as if she wanted to pretend it never happened. We all got into the habit of disappearing whenever he started. That became the pattern of our lives.

'When Sean reached sixteen, he left school and went to work in a factory in Dublin. I didn't realise it at the time, but he's told me since that he couldn't wait to get out.'

'What's he doing now?' I asked.

'Married, babby, drink, divorce. He has a drink problem. But the divorce shattered him. At last, he's admitted he has a problem and is getting help. He's been on the wagon for five months now.'

'And the others?'

'Fergus is off travelling. He's twenty-nine now, in love with an English girl, Patsy, and they're in Africa on missionary work. He'll end up in the priesthood I should think. Finn's the clever one. Gained a first-class honours degree in law. Lives in London, England, with his boyfriend.'

'Boyfriend?' I smiled as I replied. 'I bet that went down like a lump of lead with his dad.'

'Pappy never knew,' Shannon replied. 'He got lung cancer and died. Must be eleven years since. Finn was twenty-one and away at uni. He came out at the funeral. Took his boyfriend with him, a different one then, and just came straight out with it, in front of everyone. Always one to take chances, our Finn. As brazen as they come.'

'How did that go down?'

'Surprisingly well. There were a million other emotions flying around. Shock was just one more. By the end of the day, people were shaking his hand and waving politely goodbye.'

'Let me work this out,' I said. 'You must have been eighteen when your dad died. So you'd had eight years free of abuse. How did you feel about his death?'

'The same as I do now. God stepped in to save us all from him, the bastard.'

I was shocked. 'You still feel this strongly, after eleven years? No compassion, or regret?'

'After what I found out? Not an ounce,' said Shannon.

'And what was that?' I asked.

Her answer gave me goose bumps all the way up my arms. 'When Pappy left me alone, he moved on to our Maureen.'

We didn't speak any more that day. Shannon was exhausted with the effort of finally spilling it all out, and that last bit of information was too distressing for her to carry on. It sounded like she blamed herself for her dad abusing Maureen, and was not able to deal with the guilt she felt about it. I knew I couldn't press her to talk; this relationship was firmly under Shannon's control. I would have to wait.

I needn't have worried. Shannon came online at our arranged time a couple of days later.

'Hi, Jacky, the last couple of days have been good for me. It feels great talking to you.'

'That's good to hear,' I replied. 'I was worried it was proving too difficult for you.'

'Don't get me wrong,' said Shannon. 'It took a lot for me to start, but once I'd begun, it felt right. I've been like a balloon about to burst, and now instead, as I talk, I'm letting the air out and releasing my pent-up anxieties bit by bit. I don't feel as desperate as I did a week ago.'

'That's great,' I said. 'Take things at your own pace. Tell me as much or as little as you want.'

'I'm ready to talk about Maureen now,' she answered.

'Standing at the graveside, watching Pappy's coffin being lowered into the ground, I caught a glimpse of Maureen's face. She was standing very still, as if transfixed, her narrowed eyes focused intently on the coffin. The intensity of her stare alarmed me; I resolved to ask her about Pappy later on. She didn't hang around downstairs when all the relatives came back to the house. She scuttled upstairs; watching, I felt a certain empathy with her; I used to be like that once.

'And then it hit me. The realisation swept over me in waves. I used to be like that once. When Pappy was abusing me. When I was six years old. I did a quick mental calculation. He'd stopped when I was ten. That meant Maureen was . . . six. Dear God, no! "Tell me it isn't true, tell me it isn't true," I repeated over and again to myself, as I raced up the stairs after Maureen. She was fourteen now.

'I reached the top of the stairs and paused before knocking,' Shannon continued. 'Suddenly I was plagued with doubts. What if I was barking up the wrong tree? Maybe Pappy's death had hit Maureen harder than the rest of us? But on the other hand, I reasoned, what if my suspicions were true? I'd never forgive myself if I'd not tried to help her. I knocked on the door.

'We didn't go down for tea that night. We stayed awake talking, hugging, crying, grieving for our lost childhoods. Reluctant to open up initially, Maureen's eyes widened in horror when I admitted what Pappy had done to me. Yes, he had moved on to her, she said. Yes, she was terrified to say anything for fear of upsetting Mammy. Yes, he was still doing it right up to when he got really sick. And there's more. When she turned thirteen, he actually had full sex with her every fortnight.

'Now I understood why my bedtime had been extended all those years ago; it gave him a chance to be alone with Maureen. Why hadn't I seen the signs? Because I wasn't looking for them. Like I said, I was too wrapped up in my own inhibitions and anxieties to worry about anyone else.'

'Did you tell anyone at that point?' I asked.

'No,' answered Shannon. 'We both decided that we would keep it between us. He was dead now and couldn't do any more harm. If we told, we would be hurting Mammy. So, in a sick sort of way, Pappy had won again.'

I shuddered. It brought back memories for me, of when my brother-in-law had drunkenly raped me in Egypt. I had tried to speak out and tell someone. But it backfired on me terribly. No one believed me and I was beaten for suggesting such a thing. I learnt a hard lesson that day. Telling someone only made things worse. I understood Shannon perfectly.

'We'll give it a rest for today, shall we?' I suggested. 'I'm worn out.'

The following week, I logged on and was delighted that Shannon was already online waiting. She seemed to be in good spirits.

'I look forward to our chats,' she said. 'It's so easy to talk like this.'

'It's a big step,' I answered. 'We covered a lot of ground last time. Thank God you and Maureen had each other. How is she these days?'

'Maureen's twenty-four now. She suffers from depression and is on medication for it. She was never one for the boys, but met Donald when she was eighteen. He was her first serious boyfriend. They married, but it didn't last, because she couldn't stand being touched. She moved back in with me and became a virtual recluse, suffering from anxiety attacks, and cutting herself. A psychiatrist worked with her to overcome her demons, but she could not forget. Pappy ruined her life. She hasn't been able to move on, and she'll never have children of her own. She remembers the pain when he forced himself inside her, and her horror at the blood the first time. She still cries out in her sleep. If he wasn't dead, I'd kill him. But he's not the only one to blame. I should have noticed. I should have taken more care of her.'

'Shannon, you were ten years old,' I said. 'And for the last four years of your short life, you were being horrifically abused by your own father. No one could expect you to take care of anyone but yourself. You mustn't blame yourself. You've been brave and strong through all these years since. Don't take on your dad's sins as if they were your own.'

'You don't understand,' she said. 'I'm a bad person. I'm wicked.'

'How do you work that one out?' I said.

'Everyone I trust hurts me. It's always the same. I can't talk to anyone, because one day, they'll use it against me. Maureen's life wasn't the only one Pappy ruined.'

I realised that so far we hadn't actually got round to talking about how Shannon was and why she had been close to killing herself just a short while ago.

'Let's talk about you,' I suggested. 'Tell me about your life since your dad's death.'

'There was just Maureen and me living at home,' she continued. 'I'd left school at sixteen and worked at Boots the chemists. Mum was lost at first, but gradually began to relax and go out with her friends. When she brought Tom home, we were pleased for her. It was lovely hearing her laugh.

'Very quickly, he became a regular fixture at the house. I was in the bath when it happened. He walked in as if he didn't know I was there. Said he'd come for a towel. But he closed the door behind him, knelt down, put his hands under the water and tried to touch me. I screamed and jumped out, running to my room without a stitch on. Everyone heard. Mum came up to see what was going on. I pulled on a dressing-gown and sat on the bed, shaking.'

'What did Tom do?' I asked.

'He followed Mammy into my room, laughing. Said he only wanted a towel and he didn't know I was in the bath. Said he was sorry, but I should have locked the door.'

'What did your Mum do when you told her the truth about him?' I asked.

'That's just it,' answered Shannon. 'I didn't. I was too ashamed. I let him get away with it. But the old feelings came rushing back. I should have told. But I didn't.

'I could have moved out,' she continued. 'But I couldn't leave Maureen. She was still at school. I couldn't trust Tom with anyone. I used to pray every night that he would break up with Mammy, but their relationship went from strength to strength. Two years after Pappy's death, she married him. Maureen left school and I found a nice flat for the two of us to share. Mammy was grateful to have Tom to herself, so she didn't put up much of a fuss. Anyway, it was only a couple of miles away.

'Maureen found a job in a florist's, and it was there she met Donald. As for me, I went out with quite a few men, but I hated being kissed, and couldn't bear a man's face anywhere near mine if he'd had a beer. It made me shudder and want to vomit. I met Declan when I was twenty. From the start, I could feel an attraction between us, and when he kissed me, I kissed him back. He was everything that Pappy was not:

tall, clean-shaven, sweet-smelling, with soft, kind, blue eyes and light, gingery hair. I was still a virgin, and when we made love, I cried afterwards, because I didn't feel cheap or dirty. I just felt loved.'

'God bless this man,' I said. 'So you were finally able to move on?'

'It was a slow process,' she replied. 'After Maureen married Donald, Declan moved into the flat with me. That flat was my haven, where no one could get to me, where I was safe. I didn't tell Declan, but secretly I was worried that I'd feel hemmed in and anxious if we lived together. Mammy disapproved, but she got over it. Declan was a maths teacher at the local secondary school. It was his first proper job and he worked hours into the night, planning and marking work. This gave me the space I needed. All in all it worked, and we were very happy. We could tell each other anything – anything, that is, apart from my secret past. Every so often, I had a longing inside of me to tell him. But as much as I tried, I couldn't shake off Pappy's words. They went round and round in my head: if I told, Mammy would get hurt; if I told, no one would believe me; if I told, people would look down on me and think I was dirty. After all this time, he still haunted me. I still couldn't be sure how Declan would react if he knew. I might even lose him. And I wasn't about to risk that.

'Anyway, he installed a computer, connected it up to the Internet and taught me the basics. I didn't get a lot of chance to use it, as he was online most nights but, as I said, this suited me. In fact I was getting on very well with my manager, Geoff. We had the same sense of humour, neither of us was interested in the inevitable shop gossip and we took our coffee breaks together. He became a good friend, and at that point, I was the happiest I have ever been.'

'Do you realise what you're saying?' I felt I had to interrupt. 'Talking made you feel better. The more you talk, the more you relax, the more you trust.'

'That's what I was finding out,' said Shannon. 'As the months rolled on, I nearly told Declan about Pappy a million times, but chickened out at the last minute. On our second anniversary of living together, I had everything planned: candlelit dinner at a posh restaurant – well, the hotel up the road actually – back home for champagne and a heart-to-heart. Only he got there first.'

'What do you mean?'

'Oh, we had the meal all right. It wasn't exactly the most romantic of evenings. For starters, I was as twitchy as a rabbit in headlights, and he seemed tongue-tied for a change. When we got home, I produced the champagne as a surprise, but he put it on the side, took my hand and led me into the living-room. "I've got something to tell you," he said. I hardly heard him. I'd been plucking up courage all night and I was determined that this time, I would go through with it. I was going to tell him my secret. It was time. "And I've got something to tell you," I replied.

'It was weird. I wasn't really listening to him, wanting to

say my piece, and he wasn't listening to me, wanting to say his. Thank God he got in first.'

'Why? What did he have to say?' The suspense was killing me.

'His next sentence silenced me. He didn't even look me in the eye. "I've met someone else. It's serious." Turns out he'd met someone in a chat room on the net. He had no explanation, other than it had started as a friendship and grown into much more. He said it wasn't my fault. He wanted to move out.'

I couldn't believe it. 'And that was that? Didn't you fight for him?' I asked.

'I had a bit of confidence by then, but not that much,' she answered. 'I immediately blamed myself. I mean, I couldn't be that great a person if he was running off with someone he'd only talked to. No, I didn't put up a fight. I went back into my shell.

'Things moved quickly after that night,' she went on. 'Declan moved out, Maureen left Donald and moved in with me. We were both emotional wrecks, and not very good for each other. I couldn't believe I'd nearly told Declan my secret. What if I'd got in first? Would he have stayed with me out of pity? That would have been far worse. The only decent, reliable thing in my life at that point was my job. I trusted Geoff enough to tell him about my home situation and he was a great support.

'The trouble was, Declan had made me feel safe and now he wasn't there and I missed him terribly. I missed his arms around me and his kisses. I began to sink into depression. I felt helpless, as if I had no control over anything any more. I lost weight and started regressing to the behaviour of when Pappy was abusing me, being frightened to go to sleep at night, forcing my eyes to stay open and focused on the door handle.

'Strangely, it was Mammy who helped me that time. She came round on a bad day and took me off to the doctor's. I was informed that I was depressed, not to worry; everyone goes through it when there's a break-up, and given a prescription for antidepressants. They were brilliant. I wasn't so tired and, for some unknown reason, I didn't feel so bad. I started to buck up little by little. I decorated the lounge and started going out again. I slept right through the night. I began to eat sensibly. I was back.'

'Well done,' I said. 'You must have been proud of yourself.'

'Not really,' Shannon replied. 'I felt it was my duty to take care of Maureen. I had to stay stronger to be there for her. She needed me. How wrong can you be? Even she didn't want to be with me.'

'Did she meet someone?' I asked. 'If she left you for a relationship, then maybe it was for the best,' I added, taking a wild guess.

'When I emailed you for the first time,' Shannon said, 'I had just left the hospital. Maureen had taken an overdose of her pills and had lapsed into a coma. I had been sitting at her bedside for three days, trying to understand just what it was I had done or not done to make her choose this over living with me. It made everything seem worthless. It made my existence seem worthless. If she didn't want me, then what was I doing, hanging around? Everything got messed up in my head again and I became confused. I sat outside the room while Mammy and Tom were there; I still felt uncomfortable being in the same room as him and, besides, it was getting crowded. Sean and Auntie Noreen, Mammy's sister, turned up and they did shifts between them. I couldn't handle crowds. A nurse brought me a copy of your book, *Fatwa*. I devoured every word. You'd stood on that balcony, wanting to end it all, not knowing what your life was all about. Here I was, reading about someone who felt exactly the same as I did. I finished the book and turned over to the back cover, where your website address was written. I made a decision. If Maureen dies, then there's no point in me carrying on either.

'The following day, the doctor told us that Maureen's liver was failing and there was not much hope. In the midst of the ensuing mini-hysteria, I decided to go home, take an overdose and join my little sister. I put the telly on as normal, made a cup of tea, got a jug of water and a glass and emptied my pills out ready on the coffee table. I sat there for ages, oblivious to the programme, staring at the pills. The tea went cold. Finally, I logged on to your site and wrote to you via the "Ask Jacky" button. Leaving the pills on the table, I returned to the hospital.'

'It was a Saturday,' I said. 'I didn't get the message until

Monday and you said you'd wait just a day. I wrote a reply, not knowing if I was too late or not.'

'It wasn't meant to be,' replied Shannon drily. 'Maureen didn't die. She pulled through. She awoke from her coma that day. I was so certain she was going to die. I prayed and prayed, saying thank you for sparing her, and sorry for what I'd tried to do. I promised I'd never consider suicide again if Maureen pulled through. It was so uplifting to see her turn her head towards me and squeeze my hand. I was jumping for joy. For the first time in ages, I felt like confiding in someone, as if the time was right. I chose you.'

'Thank you,' I replied simply. 'I feel privileged. You are an amazing woman, Shannon.'

'There are a thousand other people in the world I would call amazing,' she replied. 'And, believe me, I'm not one of them.'

'You've taken that giant step. You've told someone your deepest, darkest secret. Me. How do you feel?'

'Honestly? Strange,' she replied. 'Too much thinking time, I suppose. I'm on my own in the flat now, you see. Mammy felt guilty that she'd not been there for Maureen. She's trying to make up for it now by looking after her while she recovers. Maureen's living there now.'

'What's the situation with Geoff these days?' I asked casually.

'Great. He's always there, interested, supportive. I don't know what I'd do without him. I've sort of known for a while that he fancies me, but he's too much of a gentleman to put pressure on me.'

I took a deep breath. 'Why don't you invite him round one evening? For a meal or something? Or go out for a drink with him?'

'He's already asked me,' Shannon said. 'But I said no.'

'Come on, Shannon, you know you didn't want to say no. It's obvious to me you trust and respect this guy. What harm can it do? Go on,' I urged. 'Reconsider.'

I was a little surprised, but highly delighted to hear from Shannon the following week. 'Hi, Jacky, I'm going out with Geoff tonight, so I can't chat for long. I want to look my best.'

'That's fantastic,' I said. 'Have a ball.'

Over the next month, contact with Shannon was rather fragmented, as she embarked on a relationship with Geoff. She would chat for five or ten minutes and then log off, eager to get on with her life. She was falling in love. I was extremely happy for her. She overcame her reservations about visiting her mother and Tom, to go and see Maureen regularly. This brought her much closer to her mother, and the three women began going out together, shopping or for walks. The tone of our chats lightened noticeably, as she relaxed in the other areas of her life. It was time to take the bull by the horns.

'Shannon, it's time.'

We had been joking about Geoff's romantic gestures, the little notes he left for her to find.

'Time? Time for what?' she asked.

'This is the big one. Geoff is it for you, isn't he?' I pressed.

'I hope so,' came the reply.

'Then doesn't he deserve to know? Not everyone who knows will use it against you,' I persisted. 'Like me, for instance.'

'I don't want to lose him. He'd be shocked. He'd see me in a different light. I hear what you're saying, Jacky, and you're probably right. But I've coped alone for so many years. I'd be embarrassed and ashamed.'

'I know,' I replied. 'And you've done brilliantly. But you're not on your own now. And if Geoff means that much to you, he deserves to know who you really are. Look at how far you've come after telling me. Tell Geoff and you can rule the world together.' I crossed my fingers as I waited for her reply. A minute later, her answer flashed up on the screen:

'You're right. I'm being silly. I've got to do this. I'll tell him tonight.'

Shannon left an email for me the following day, asking me to log on that evening at six.

'It was nerve-wracking, but I did it. I was terrified. I've never been as close to anyone as I am to Geoff, and I didn't want to lose him. I suppose telling him put the whole relationship on trial. But it was worth it. It all came spilling out. Geoff sat quietly, rocking me in his arms, and we cried together. He's the most wonderful man in the world. I love him, Jacky.'

'I'm so happy for you,' I replied. 'You can move on now.'

'It won't be easy,' Shannon replied. 'We talked long into the night. Geoff's trying to convince me to tell Mammy, not just for my sake, but for Maureen's too. He says, if Maureen feels Mammy knows and will be there for her, maybe she can move on and begin to build a life for herself too.'

'And what did you say?' I asked.

'I didn't say no,' she replied. 'I'm thinking. It's all a bit much at the moment. Geoff said he'd be by my side the whole time. He wants us to tell Maureen I've told him and let her get used to that. Then we can tell Mammy together. The three of us.'

'Sounds like a good idea to me,' I said. 'You're getting on well with your mum at the moment. Maybe this would be the best time. Go for it, Shannon.'

Geoff was a gift from God to Shannon. Shannon had enough faith in his love and support to confront Maureen alone and gently lead her through the events of the last couple of months. She then brought Geoff into the room, to help Maureen see with her own eyes that Shannon had told someone their secret after all these years.

'It was a very emotional moment,' Shannon told me. 'Maureen went through fear, disbelief and panic, before collapsing into my arms and sobbing her heart out. Geoff had to keep repeating that he believed us. She was totally bewildered. I can see now that it was totally the right thing to do. She had all this buried inside her, just like me. The effort of keeping it a secret prevented us both from getting on with anything else.'

'There's help out there, you know,' I said. 'You don't have to get through this on your own. Now you've told Geoff, you could think about counselling. They're trained and everything that passes between you is confidential.'

'Thanks, Jacky, but we need to tell Mammy first.'

It was a month before Maureen felt ready to confront their mother. This time, Geoff was present from the beginning. They made sure Tom was out.

'Mammy was horrified,' Shannon said. 'She was terribly upset. Of course she didn't want to believe us but, looking at the state of us both, she knew in her heart how hard it was for us to speak out, and that every word we uttered was true. She began blaming herself that she hadn't picked up on it. She was shattered. We cried and told each other how much we cared. Like you, Mammy suggested we both go for counselling. She said she could arrange it for us.'

'That's great news, I said. 'Are you both okay with that?'

'We're determined to give it a try,' she replied. 'If it doesn't work out, we've still got each other. After all,' she added. 'What good can a stranger do?'

'I was a stranger,' I replied quietly.

'We go every week. Mine's called Ginny and Maureen's is Debbie.' Initially sceptical, Shannon was now brimming with enthusiasm about the counsellors.

'When I first started to talk, I couldn't help it, I burst into tears. I thought she'd be annoyed but, instead, she put her hand on my shoulder, offered me a tissue and encouraged me to keep talking. A complete stranger was watching me make a fool of myself and not laughing. I couldn't believe she wanted to listen, that she would be interested.

'It was the same for Maureen,' Shannon went on. 'We're beginning to realise that it was us who had the problem, not other people. We're gradually accepting our past. I've even stopped feeling ashamed. You were right, Jacky. You can only move on if you let it out. Only then can we stop being the victim.'

Shannon and I are still in touch. She is making wonderful progress, surrounded by a solid support network. Like me, she has made herself visible again.

17

Tamara

As part of my research for this book, I sent out an invitation on my website for women to write in with their stories. It was in this way that I became acquainted with Tamara. Her email was certainly an attention-grabber. It said, 'Dear Ms Trevane, I think I am on the verge of going mad. I have an involuntary urge to scream, so that someone might hear me, or even acknowledge my existence. I haven't done it yet, but I'm very close. I am in hell, and there is no one to talk to. My situation may or may not be appropriate for your book but, either way, if you merely bother to reply, then you will be the first person in a long time to pay me attention.' She had signed it, 'Yours sincerely, Tamara Hunt.'

Interesting. There was no way I could ignore this. I was in no particular position to offer this complete stranger any help any more than the next person. But here she was, sending me her SOS. I was just getting ready to go to my daughter Leila's house to baby-sit and didn't really have time for a long session, but I couldn't resist a little reply.

'Dear Tamara,' I replied, 'I hear you loud and clear. Scream away if you want to.'

I don't know what I was expecting. By now, after all the women I'd become involved with, you'd have thought I was beyond surprise. Yet her answer did indeed surprise me.

'Screaming for me is more serious than most. I would really be in self-destruct mode if I started on that track. I'm an opera singer, you see.'

I smiled. Her reply provoked the ridiculous image of a busty diva tucked up in bed with a sore throat. 'She's probably one of those dramatic types who fall apart if someone in the chorus doesn't turn up for rehearsal,' I thought.

I didn't reply straightaway. Assuming she was a bit of a drama queen, I figured I had more important things to attend to. My gaze fell on the clock on the desk. Was that really the time? I was due at Leila's in fifteen minutes!

'I don't know why you get so involved, Mum. You could get yourself into serious trouble one of these days.' I was sitting in the front room, watching my granddaughter, Chloe, brush the tail of Barbie's pony.

Leila pulled on her coat and gave me a quick kiss. 'You're not qualified to give any of these women advice, and what would happen if they acted on what you'd said and something dreadful happened? It could all backfire on you.'

Warming my hands around my mug of tea, I nodded ruefully. I knew she was right. 'I know, darling. Sometimes I say the wrong things and I could kick myself. I'm not always as sympathetic as I could be, and often too harsh with my judgments. I can see I'm going to have to tread a lot more carefully in future.'

Leila picked Chloe up and planted a big kiss on her cheek. 'Look after Nanny for me, poppet. Mummy'll be back soon.'

'No, Nanny, let me.'

Chloe took the book away from me and proceeded to read it herself, making up a wonderful story to the pictures, far better than the print on the pages. At three, she was becoming very independent.

'There. Did you like it, Nanny? Can we change Baby Annabel now?'

Baby Annabel was the doll of the moment, complete with nappies, pushchair and changing mat. Just watching Chloe happily and confidently handling the doll and tucking her into the pushchair made me shiver inwardly with emotion. We were so lucky. How different things would have been if we had stayed in Egypt.

Leila's words resounded in my head, 'It could all backfire on you.' What if she were right? What if, by some strange quirk of fate, someone from Egypt was able to trace us from me talking to these women around the world? Or if I angered one of them by a thoughtless comment and they turned against me? I was going to have to take things much more seriously.

Back home, I logged on, deciding to contact Tamara and give her the brush-off. A few hours had gone by since her email. Whatever the problem had been, it would probably have been solved and replaced by another, equally dramatic one by now.

'Hello Tamara,' I wrote. 'I hope things have sorted

themselves out now. Although I can listen to you, I can't offer you any advice or anything. I'm just a sympathetic ear, no more, no less. There must be people closer to you who would understand you much better than I.'

'You'd be surprised,' came the reply. 'I thought I had a large circle of friends who would automatically step in with support, or just "a sympathetic ear", as you call it. Not one of my so-called friends has been there for me, not even to listen. Of course, that's not what they'd say. They all put on sad faces and pat me on the back and say they'll pop round. But the phone stays silent, and no one has actually come round. If I meet anyone by chance, they are full of hollow promises about getting in touch. No one has. I can't understand it. If I tell you all about me, maybe you'll be able to enlighten me.'

I sighed. What to do? However trivial her problems, if I, a total stranger, were to turn her down, she would feel totally rejected. I didn't want to be the one to send her on the quick route to depression. Surely it wouldn't hurt just to listen?

'Ready when you are,' I typed, 'and please, call me Jacky.' I left the computer and went to prepare tea.

I awoke the next morning to bright, blue skies with the sun streaming through the window. After Ben and Adam had left, I showered and dressed in record time, anxious to get out with Henry before the weather changed its mind. It had been raining almost non-stop for the past fortnight. I was fed up to the back teeth with windy, wet, muddy walks, not to mention Henry, who had perfected a miraculous twice-daily transformation. From cocker spaniel to large, bedraggled rat within minutes. My patience was sorely tested on our return when he lovingly shook half a puddle all over the pale maple kitchen units and sat waiting for me to towel him dry, wagging his tail in glee.

Today, however, we might be able to snatch a dry walk. Hooray! Quickly, I looked in my Inbox to see that Tamara had written a lengthy letter. I printed it off to take along. There was more than one advantage to a dry day. I could sit on a bench and read, while Henry played with his canine friends in the park. Perfect.

Henry wasted no time. He quickly hooked up with a lively little Jack Russell, and within minutes they were tearing round and round in frenzied circles, barking delightedly. I removed the letter from my pocket, settled down and began to read.

'I live with my husband, Oliver, and son, Josh, in Chelsea, London. I'm thirty-five, Oliver forty-two and Josh is four. We have an apartment in Florida and a villa in Switzerland. Oliver is a film director; he's just finished his third film. I used to sing professionally full-time and was in good demand, but nowadays I take on a lot less. My agent takes care of all that for me and makes sure I only sing in one production a year. I've had to cut personal appearances and private functions down to a minimum. How our lives have changed.'

I was puzzled. Why was she telling me all this? I'd assumed

she was annoyed about a trivial matter, would moan on about it for a bit, get it off her chest, and that would be that. For all that, it certainly is interesting, I mused. They must be well-off to maintain three properties. And only one child? A life in the bright lights of entertainment and the film industry? Lucky lady. I read on.

'Five years ago, we were a successful couple, both in the limelight in our own right, at the peak of our respective careers. Our social calendar was constantly overflowing. Together, Oli and I made a great team; we had independent, busy schedules, yet always made the effort to consider one another. When apart, we spoke daily and took an interest in each other's day. I suppose we had similar ambitious streaks and there was a strong mutual respect for that between us.

'We got married in a beautiful Scottish castle ten years ago, after a two-year engagement. I was twenty-five. I knew Oli was "the one", but I had so many dreams to follow, I wasn't ready to rush into marriage and a family. He was great about it, actively encouraging me to tour with operatic societies and build up a decent portfolio. When we finally made a date and went ahead with the marriage, I was the happiest woman in the world.

'The next couple of years passed in the blink of an eye. Oliver directed his first film, which did well, resulting in trips away, interviews and business meetings. He went into partnership with a Swiss film producer for his next film. We spent so much time over there, we ended up buying a villa. The ski season is always fantastic; Oliver was constantly

248

surrounded by rich friends, so the social life continued apace, no matter where we were living.

'It was on a trip to Milan, where I met a fellow opera singer, Maria, that I made up my mind to try for a baby. She had certainly lived a colourful life, travelling all over the world, and had made three CDs to date. Her passion for singing had been all-consuming, however; she lived within a social whirl of engagements and dinner parties, found herself in and out of several lovers' beds in various cities, permanently on the high-life treadmill. Now, at the grand old age of forty-eight, she was looking a little frayed around the edges. As we sat in our hotel at nine a.m., awaiting a car to take us to rehearsal, I saw how blinding passion could be. Glass of champagne in her hand, Maria entertained me with intimate details of her current Latin lover. One day soon, time would catch up with her, and singing would no longer be the focus of her life. And then what? I didn't want to end up like that.

'I returned from that trip, longing to start a family with Oli and to plan for a future that included the patter of tiny feet. He was delighted. I remember him sweeping me into his arms and dancing out into the street. It was what he had always hoped for, yet would never have pushed for unless the time was right for me too.'

That was it. The end of her email. I pushed it into my pocket and called Henry to walk back home. The dry weather was holding out, although there was a band of cloud gathering to the west. I dawdled all the way, enjoying the fresh air, smiling as Henry took advantage of my slow gait to mark every gatepost along the way. I pondered the contents of Tamara's email. What was her problem exactly? All that reading and I still was none the wiser. I knew I wouldn't be able to leave things at that. I knew I'd have to get involved. I knew too much to stop now. I knew I was probably making a foolish decision. But I also knew it was the only decision to make.

The next afternoon, Saturday, I found myself miraculously with a couple of hours to spare. Another dry day, Ben and his dad had gone off to play golf and I'd just dropped Adam at his friend's house.

'Here we go, then,' I whispered, sitting at the computer, eager to know more.

'Hello, Tamara. I'm intrigued. Sounds like you had an enviable lifestyle a few years ago. Has it all gone wrong somehow?'

I sent the message, but then had doubts. 'That was far too direct,' I thought. 'I should have let her tell me. I'm not very good at this.' I sat there impatiently for ten minutes, after which Tamara sent her reply.

'I really don't know why I'm telling you all this,' she wrote. 'Now I've found someone to listen to me, it's hard for me to spill it all out. I'm a very emotional person, and ended up sobbing uncontrollably while writing the last letter. I simply couldn't go on.'

She needed reassurance. I was happy to give it.

'Tamara, write anything you want, at any time and I will listen,' I replied. 'There again, if you feel you can't, then that's okay too. We can use MSN-messaging, if it's easier for you. It's up to you.'

Tamara was more than willing to chat on MSN. It made our emails more real, getting instant replies and seeing the whole conversation on the screen. We could interrupt one another, or take time out. Ultimately, this arrangement proved to be a much more satisfactory one.

'I suppose I'm finding it so difficult because in telling you, I'm remembering how it used to be,' she wrote. 'Honestly, Jacky, we were so happy. So bloody happy.'

I wanted her to move on and get to the point. 'You'd just decided to have children,' I began. 'What happened then?'

'Nothing. That was the problem,' she replied. 'We had great fun trying to make babies, but it didn't happen. The doctor could find nothing wrong. Eventually after eighteen months, I fell pregnant. We were overjoyed, rushing out to buy prams, car seats and Babygros. I was actually choosing the wallpaper for the nursery when the pains started. Right there in the shop. I lost our baby at twelve weeks.'

I was stunned. 'Poor you,' was all I could write. Then, as an afterthought, 'How did you cope?'

'Oliver withdrew and immersed himself in his work. The one time I really needed him, he wasn't there. We didn't discuss it. I fell apart. It was so public, you see. Everybody knew I was pregnant, yet we didn't broadcast the fact that I'd lost the baby. I kept having to tell people, every time they asked, how I was. I couldn't stand it. A couple of months later, we left for Switzerland, and it was there that I discovered I was pregnant again. We were more careful this time. Didn't tell a soul. I immediately stopped skiing, returned to Chelsea and took it easy. I lost that baby at ten weeks.'

I felt sick. Suddenly Tamara's world had been turned upside down. 'It must have been terrible for you both.'

'It was. After agonising together for days on end, we both decided to stop trying to get pregnant. We booked a holiday in Barbados, to spend quality time together and face up to things when we got back. I was planning on going back on the pill. There were other avenues to explore – adoption, fostering, even IVF – but neither of us was ready to go there yet.'

'Did you manage to wind down on the holiday?'

'It was tearful, emotional, and precious,' Tamara answered. 'But at least we found each other again, and we were closer than ever. What I didn't realise until several weeks later was that I had conceived again on that holiday. So our plans were immediately scuppered. This time, I was resigned to the fact that I wouldn't get past three months. I even tried to prepare myself for the grief that was to come. I took things very easy, staying in bed until lunch-time and not going out. At four months, I couldn't believe the baby was still alive. Still, we told no one. At twenty weeks, I felt him move inside me. I was overcome. It is a feeling I will cherish forever. Josh was born three weeks premature, and there were no prouder parents in the world than Oliver and me.'

'That's wonderful,' I said. 'An heir to the Hunt empire. And hopefully lots more to follow.'

'There won't be any brothers or sisters for Josh, I'm afraid.'

Me and my big mouth. I swore silently, annoyed that once again I'd said the wrong thing. The birth had probably been traumatic, she could have had complications and been told she couldn't have any more children. I decided to try and laugh it off. Big mistake.

'Why not? Is Josh too much of a handful?' I joked.

The answer stunned me into silence. 'Basically, yes.'

I was digging myself deeper and deeper into a hole. 'I'm really sorry, Tamara. I seem to have the knack of saying the wrong thing at the wrong time. I was trying to make light of the situation. But in doing that, I've made everything worse. Just talk and I'll listen.'

'You know, the irony is that if it wasn't true, we would be laughing at that now,' she replied. 'The first-born is always a steep learning curve for us, isn't it? Parents for the first time, suddenly responsible for a new little being. He was so very, very precious, you see. I suppose I was obsessed with him, checking that he was still breathing every fifteen minutes, despite having a portable baby alarm attached to my belt. He was my little miracle. All our friends oohed and aahed at appropriate moments, but every one of them has live-in nannies and au pairs. I couldn't bear to be apart from Josh. Despite Oliver's attempts to persuade me to take time out and hire a nanny, I wasn't ready at first. I wanted to be the one who was there for him.'

'How did Oliver respond to fatherhood?' I asked.

'Fine. He was over the moon at the birth and adores Josh. He even changed a few nappies. To be honest, he's not around that much to be as supportive as I would like. On the surface, he supported my decision to be a full-time mum but, underneath, I think he agreed with our friends. During those first few months he was merely indulging me, hoping it was a phase that I'd eventually get over and then, "get on with my life". But to me, this *was* my life now.'

We had the baby shower after the birth,' she went on. 'As no one knew about the pregnancy, I didn't do all the traditional things before the birth. So many friends turned up with kisses, congratulations and presents. They spent five minutes cooing over Joshua, and then expected someone to "appear" and whisk him away, so we could get on with the party. After all, that was the way it was supposed to be. I think it was as far back as that very day that I began losing some of my friends. I didn't fit in any more.'

'What do you mean?' I asked.

'The people we mixed with were all rich, famous or both. Generally speaking, they had a lifestyle that revolved around image, functions and publicity. They and their egos were the centre of their own worlds. Children were not supposed to alter their image; hence the nannies for the "dirty bits". It was as if they were in the way, brought out occasionally to be shown off. I'd lost two babies before Josh. When he arrived, he became the most important person in the world to me.

My needs were inconsequential. Funny, I'd never seen anything wrong in the way we all were. Until then.

'Now, looking back, I suppose I noticed something wasn't quite right in the first six months,' she continued. 'I devoured all the baby books and parenting magazines, watching for Josh to display the usual developmental signs. But even at a few months old, he didn't seem to recognise me. He smiled, but never at the sound of my voice or if I picked him up. I had a nagging feeling that I wasn't doing it right, that he didn't like me.'

'Sounds like you were so anxious to get it right, you were looking for things to go wrong,' I offered. 'Wasn't there anyone around to reassure you?'

'The truth is, Josh never settled into a regular sleeping pattern. He woke every hour, with his high-pitched scream, and didn't stop when I picked him up. I tried everything, even leaving him to cry. It was a sorry sight; him wailing in his cot and me crying with frustration outside the door. The health visitor assumed I was exaggerating. She said I was to make sure he was dry, comfortable and fed, put him to bed, switch off the light and leave him. It didn't work. Nothing did. I was worn out. I got into the habit of cat-napping, just to survive.'

'Leila, my first child, cried a lot,' I said, in an effort to make her feel better. 'It took her a good three months to sleep through the night.'

'At six months, I had lost over a stone in weight, and was trying to wean him off the breast. If he hadn't had that, I'm sure he would have died, because he wouldn't take solids at all. Eventually, at ten months, I managed to wean him. What a battle! And it didn't stop there. From the day he was born, we had showered him with cuddly toys, rattles and pretty mobiles, and hung bright pictures in his nursery to stimulate him. I read stories daily and pushed toy trains along the border of the carpet. He was never interested in any of them, unless it was to put them in his mouth. Gradually, I was feeling a failure. There must be something I wasn't doing. His behaviour didn't seem normal, although I couldn't actually say what was wrong.'

'What did your friends think?' I asked.

'That's the other thing. As far as my friends were concerned, Joshua was a normal, healthy boy with a neurotic mummy. They never involved themselves much with the daily grind of child-rearing, and hadn't noticed if their child had smiled directly at them, or if they had played with baby toys. I was paranoid, they said. I should admit defeat, get a nanny and chill out, they said. I hardly saw any of my friends any more, because Josh took up all my time. Rather than offering their support, they chose to withdraw and let me "get on with it".'

'So you were barely coping, and doing all this on your own?' I asked.

'Exactly,' she replied. 'Oliver was very involved with his current film and spending a fair amount of time in Switzerland. I stayed here in Chelsea, thinking that a change in routine for Josh would only make things worse. Oliver would fly back for weekends or even odd days to see how we were doing. He did as much as he could and I always put on a brave face. If I admit it, I really needed him to be there on a day-to-day basis. He didn't see me struggling or sense my gradual decline. I think fatherhood went to Oliver's head. I know he can be extravagant, but he did go a little OTT for Josh's first Christmas. He bought an apartment in Florida, so Josh could see Mickey Mouse whenever he liked!

'When Josh was six months old,' she continued, 'Oliver persuaded me to go out to dinner. We hired a baby-sitter, but Josh screamed and cried the whole time. The poor girl was so distressed, she refused to sit again for us. I knew then that any hopes I had had to return to my singing career were not on the cards. Not for a while, anyway.'

'Do you have any time off? What about nursery school, or toddler group? That would give you a break,' I suggested.

'As soon as Oliver had registered Josh's birth, he put his name down for St Martin's, a brilliant public school only a short drive away. They have a wonderful nursery with excellent facilities. I took Josh twice. Each time, he quickly became engaged in playing with the toy telephone. He loves punching the numbers and watching them light up. It was such a relief, watching him play normally. The first day, I left him after half an hour. When I returned two hours later to pick him up, it was a different story. Mrs Murray, the teacher, said that Josh had not played with the other children, and refused to share the telephone. When she had tried to reason with him, he had had a tantrum, shouting, screaming and kicking. He would not respond to his name, she said. She asked if Josh was used to playing with other children. I couldn't tell her that no one wanted to play with him any more, and he wasn't invited to any more birthday parties because of his tantrums. I merely shook my head. Mrs Murray suggested I bring him and stay with him in the future, until he was ready to be left on his own. I tried that the following day. When another little girl picked up the telephone, he flew into a rage and hit her with it. Then he wet himself, all over the floor. We haven't been back. He'll be five in August. How will we cope with proper school? I'm at my wit's end.'

It was obvious that Tamara had had a rough ride. She was describing herself as alone, putting on a brave face, hiding her true feelings, scared of not coping. She was an invisible woman who needed help. But Josh was four years old now, wasn't he? Surely she hadn't been battling it out alone for the past four years?

I thought back to when I had lived in Egypt, when I was trying desperately to cope and knowing that I wasn't coping. It got so bad that if he didn't like the food I had cooked, my husband, Omar, would throw it on the floor and make me lick it up. I never told anyone. I took the aggression and the beatings submissively and, but for the girls, would probably still be battling it out there now. Yes, I could identify pretty well with how Tamara was feeling.

'Tell me more about Josh,' I wrote. 'How you've managed until now.'

'Gradually, as Josh grew, his temper tantrums grew with him,' she answered. 'He would become interested in something – Oliver's torch, for example – and would spend hours clicking it on and off, on and off, giving it his full attention. If I called his name, he didn't respond, or even look at me. If I dared to try and take the torch away so that we could have tea, he would flare up angrily, screaming and kicking out. Even now, he will sit on the floor in a corner and rock, backwards and forwards, humming, as if he is in his own little world. He doesn't speak much either; at four, he can barely string a sentence together. In all that time, he has never once locked eyes with me and smiled. I have an ache inside me, willing him to look up, smile and tell me he loves me.'

Reading this last entry stirred something inside me. It was as if someone had switched on a light. I typed quickly, 'Tamara, don't go away. I have to make a phone call. I have an idea.'

Ten minutes later, I was back online with Tamara. 'Hi there. Sorry about that. It's just that, I think there might be light at the end of the tunnel for you, so to speak.'

Tamara didn't sound convinced. 'How? How can there be a solution to this? It's obvious that some people are born to be mothers and others are not. No matter how much I want to be in the first category, I'm finally coming round to accepting that I am most firmly in the second. I can't do motherhood.'

'Tamara, have you ever voiced any of your concerns about

Josh to anyone else?' I asked. 'Oliver maybe, or the doctor?'

'Oli sees Josh when he has tantrums. It's hard to avoid; he has so many. So far, I've managed to give him the impression that Josh is tired or moody. He's never around for long periods, you see. If he knew Josh was always like that, he'd see what a bad mother I was. I don't think I could cope with that. As for the doctor, every time we've been, Josh has behaved brilliantly. He has a fascination with calculators, and the doctor has a large one on his desk. Josh sits there as good as gold, punching in the numbers over and again. I can't very well admit that he's terrible at home after such a display of angelic behaviour, can I?'

I was excited as I wrote my reply. 'Actually, I think that's exactly what you need to do. It sounds to me as if Josh may be autistic. The more you try to cope alone, the more frustrated you'll become. There's help to be had out there, you know. And more importantly,' I added, 'Josh's behaviour is not down to your poor skills as a mother. It's all about him, not you. There's nothing for you to feel bad about.'

I sat there, impatiently waiting for her response. I was sure I'd hit the nail on the head. My friend, Helen, worked with children with special needs, and had an autistic son of her own. Although autism varies widely from child to child, some of Josh's behaviour struck a chord with me: his fixations, his rocking, his lack of eye contact. Helen agreed that it was very likely he was autistic. I was ecstatic. There was hope on the horizon.

Finally, Tamara answered. 'No, Jacky. You've jumped to

the wrong conclusion. I didn't know what autism was, so I've just looked it up. If there's one thing I am sure of, it is this: my son is not retarded. I need to go now. We'll chat later.'

I had shocked her; that much was obvious. She didn't believe me, or more likely, didn't *want* to believe me. I had confronted her with a completely new concept by suggesting that there was a valid reason for Josh's behaviour. It wasn't down to bad parenting. She was off the hook.

I was a little surprised by her reaction. I myself was so excited that I kind of expected her to mirror my feelings and jump for joy. But the more I thought about it, the more I understood. It was one thing to accept that you were not responsible for your son's behaviour. It was quite another to take on board that there was a label that could be attached to him. It was simply too much for her to absorb, so she was dismissing it. For now.

I couldn't leave it at that. All my instincts told me to leave her to mull everything over. But I had to reply. She had gone offline, so I emailed her instead. 'Tamara, if Josh has problems coping with our world, then he isn't retarded. It just means you can make a start in trying to help him. I'll see what I can find out from my end. But please, don't dismiss what I've said without a second thought. Speak to Oliver.' As an afterthought, I added, 'There's no shame in being autistic, you know.'

The rest of the weekend passed in a whirl of shopping, cleaning, playing chauffeur to Adam and having a dinner party for eight. It had been unusual for me to sit at the computer for the whole of a Saturday afternoon; consequently I had to rush to fit everything in. The next week passed with no word from Tamara. For my part, I visited Helen, who gave me lots of practical advice to pass on to Tamara when she got in touch.

'Whatever you do, don't rush her,' warned Helen. 'By the sound of it, Tamara and Oliver's relationship changed the instant they became parents and Tamara made the controversial decision to be a full-time mother. Having a child who requires more attention and care places an even greater strain on that relationship. She must be completely overwhelmed.'

'I know,' I replied. 'She'll be fighting with her emotions, now I've thrown this spanner into the works. She'll go through the lot: shock and disbelief, denial – that's where she's at now – then anger and confusion and probably guilt, shame, fear and panic. Then I can try and encourage her to seek help and she'll start to accept it. I do hope she discusses things with Oliver and they can face this as a couple.'

'Remember,' said Helen as I left, 'don't nag her. Let her contact you, no matter how frustrating it is. She needs to do this bit herself.'

When another week went by with no word from Tamara, I was crawling the walls in suspense. As each day passed, I would think, 'She'll be in touch tomorrow.' But now, too many days had gone by and my confidence was sagging. I decided to give her another week and then contact her myself, just to say hello.

The next morning, there was an email from Tamara in my Inbox. 'Jacky, I'll be online at six this evening. Hope you're free to chat.'

I certainly was. At six o'clock sharp, I was at the computer, waiting. She came online at five past.

'Hi, Jacky. How are you?'

'Hello, Tamara. I'm fine. It's so good to hear from you. How are you feeling?'

'Better. We have some important news.'

'We?'

'Yes, Oliver, Josh and I.'

I was thrilled. Tamara must have confided in Oliver after all. Good girl. They were working together as a family unit. A huge step in the right direction. I decided to make sure.

'That's great, Tamara,' I said. 'You spoke to him then?'

'Yes. Frankly, I was shocked when you suggested that Josh might be autistic. I couldn't believe it; no, I absolutely refused to believe it at first. Yet no matter how much I pushed the idea to the back of my mind, it kept returning and bothering me. Then, when I couldn't seem to dismiss these foreign, unwanted thoughts from my head, I became angry. And I'm sorry to say this, but I focused every ounce of that anger on you, Jacky. I was furious, livid, out of my mind with rage that you could suggest that my son was not perfect. It all built up inside me, and when Oliver came home for the weekend and Josh didn't turn round when he called him, I decided I wasn't going to hide the truth any more.'

I heaved a huge sigh of relief. 'Well done, Tamara.'

'I was desperate, you see,' she said. 'When all my anger had cooled off, I felt suddenly confused and helpless. And most of all, I felt alone. Completely invisible. Now, more than ever, I needed to tell someone, and for that someone to understand me and hold my hand and tell me that I wasn't going mad and that things would be okay. So I sat down with Oliver and a large glass of Merlot. And I told him about Josh. The real Josh. Our son.'

'How did he react?'

'It was the weirdest thing. He wasn't that surprised. In fact, when I'd told him absolutely everything, he seemed almost relieved. And when I told him your thoughts on Josh being autistic, he became animated and optimistic. Can you believe it?'

'Yes, yes, yes,' I said. 'I only wish you'd talked to him earlier.'

'Do you know, that's exactly what Oli said. He has always had the feeling that I wanted Josh all to myself and wouldn't let him in. But it wasn't like that at all. I didn't want to make an even bigger fool of myself by showing him what a failure I was in handling Josh.'

'And it all backfired on you, didn't it?' I said.

'I've learnt my lesson. I'm frightened for Josh and panic sometimes when he plays up, but I've come round to the idea that he would benefit from professional help.'

'Good for you.'

'We've been busy since we last talked,' she continued. 'Josh has had an assessment and has been diagnosed as autistic. Somehow, having professionals recognise the symptoms makes it easier for me to bear. Oliver has spent a lot of time looking for resources and dealing with the service providers. It's all a bit too much for me. My hands are full looking after Josh. Oliver still leaves Josh to me, although he is with me in spirit. He's always ringing to see how I'm coping and reassuring me that I'm doing well. You were right, Jacky. Maybe there is light at the end of that tunnel after all.'

'Of course there is. I feel proud that you found the strength to reach out to Oliver. It was the best thing you could have done.'

Her response was swift. 'It was the only thing left to do.'

During the next few months, Tamara and Oliver entered a different world. A world where the child and his special needs were the primary concern. A world where nothing was certain, nothing guaranteed, nothing promised. Instead of St Martin's, Josh was enrolled in a special school, a state school. A school with trained, caring professionals, offering support and providing a strict routine in Josh's life. An alien world indeed to both Tamara and Oliver. Slowly, they learnt about Josh's world. Simultaneously, they learnt about special needs education and the wealth of provision on offer. They joined a local support group and met others facing similar fears and feelings of helplessness. Tamara kept me up to date on a weekly basis; we would have 'coffee and biscuits' together, on Friday mornings at ten-thirty. What we actually did was chat online as usual, but with coffee and a couple of digestives. But we called it our coffee break.

As the weeks rolled by, I saw less and less of the old, desperate Tamara. A new Tamara was beginning to emerge; one with hope in her heart and enthusiasm for the future.

'It's really encouraging listening to other families with similar struggles,' she said, one Friday morning. 'Some of them have been through hell. I thought I was the only mother in the world to have a son like Josh. But in fact autism now affects half a million people in the UK. Did you know that?'

'I guessed there would be a lot,' I said. 'The support network is vast and all over the country. Help for Josh wouldn't be so readily available if there were only a few incidences.'

'Oliver and I are committed to attending sessions with a counsellor as well,' she continued. 'Only once a month, but together with the local support group, we should be well on our way to coping.'

'You actually sound as if you are enjoying this experience,' I commented.

'Do you know, the more we learn, the more we want to know,' Tamara replied. 'It's absolutely fascinating. Autistic children are born with immature brain development in the limbic system and cerebellum. That's why Josh seemed to be on another planet. He was withdrawing into "his" world.

We are learning how to coax him out of his world and into ours. Otherwise, if he withdraws, there's a chance that other parts of his brain are not going to develop properly.'

'How is Josh responding?' I asked.

'It's remarkable, and all thanks to you, Jacky.'

'Me? What did I do? You're the one who is turning her life around. I hardly recognise you, Tamara,' I replied.

'You're right,' she said. 'I *am* different. I feel stronger, I smile more often, I even look different. I had let myself go considerably, I must confess. And if you hadn't offered me your "sympathetic ear", as you call it, I would still be the dowdy, desperate housewife, heading for tragedy. It was you who made me look beyond myself, and consider that not everything was as a result of my failings. It was you who introduced me to autism. I would even go as far as to say that Josh owes his life to you. Early diagnosis is critical apparently. The earlier the disorder is discovered, the better the prognosis. We can get to work on all Josh's skills – language, motor, visual – as well as his social behaviour and intellectual abilities, because we have now identified and accepted his limitations.'

'That's great,' I replied. 'By the way, Josh will be five next week. Are you celebrating?'

'He's having a party. Six children will be coming, all with different special needs. And I'm not dreading it at all. The parents at the centre are lovely people and I've made some good friends. Sometimes I look back at the friends I used to have and I know whom I'd rather have. I can see now how shallow they are. Their friendship was just as shallow. Give me the genuine carers any day.'

What Tamara didn't realise was that, a few short years ago, she had been one of those shallow people, who was extremely happy with her lot. 'Ignorance is bliss,' I thought. Now she looks at them with understanding and pity. I liked the new Tamara. Her enthusiasm was infectious, as she told me of Josh's progress.

'Now Josh has started speech and occupational therapy, his speech development has soared,' she said. 'If I'd only known how dangerous it was to let Josh sit and rock the way he did. You have got to keep autistic children engaged with the world. He was rocking so he could shut the world out. There's an explanation for his screaming, too. He knew what he wanted to say and became so frustrated at not being able to say it, he simply screamed.'

'How is he at home?' I asked.

'A thousand times better, and it's all because we are understanding him more every day,' she said. 'For instance, we've just found out that the fluorescent lights in the kitchen bother him dreadfully. We had special spotlights fitted with dimmer switches and he will now sit quietly and eat dinner with us. There's no magic wand on this journey. We're literally feeling our way through. Mealtimes are improving. To get him to eat something he's not keen on, I tell him that if he has a small portion of it, then he can have his baked beans. He loves baked beans. It's working.'

In fact, Tamara's life in general was now working. They

took Josh to Florida for Christmas and returned happy and relaxed. Tamara refreshed her relationship with her agent and took on a few local engagements.

'Josh is a wonderful singer. He has the voice of an angel,' she told me one day. 'He has perfect pitch and can hum back a tune after hearing it only once. He loves me practising and we spend a lot of time together rehearsing for my concerts.'

It was now obvious that Tamara loved being with Josh and she loved him for who he was. She was completely happy with her lot. As for me, I made the decision to put down my pen and concentrate on being happy with mine.

One year on, Tamara contacted me, bursting with anticipation. 'Hi, Jacky, are you there? I can't wait to tell you.'

'Hi, there. What's new?' I asked.

'We're pregnant!' she said. 'I'm five months gone now and feeling great.'

'Congratulations,' I said, delighted for her. 'What does Josh think about it?'

'He'll understand better when she arrives,' answered Tamara. 'But we keep talking about her to him. We've already given her a name so he can get used to it.'

'Name? Her?' I was baffled.

'I had a scan yesterday and it's a girl. Isn't that marvellous? Harriet. What do you think? We both love that name.'

Harriet was born two days late. Tamara wasted no time in telling me all about her. 'This time, I'll be on the lookout for signs,' she said. 'If there's anything wrong with Harriet, I'll soon know.'

I admired her tenacity and strength of character. Unrecognisable from her vulnerable, former self, she was now prepared for anything that the future had in store.

'At the moment she cries to be fed and quietens when I feed her. I would describe that as normal so far,' said Tamara.

'How would you describe Josh these days?' I asked casually.

'Just as I always do,' came the swift reply. 'Perfect.'

Acknowledgements

To all the brave women who have taken that step to speak out and selflessly let me write their stories, God bless you. Let's hope we can help others to do the same.

To my friend and mentor, Clifford Thurlow, a huge bear hug. You taught me how to write from the heart with style. You gave me the confidence to go it alone, and willingly stepped back to let me get on with it. For that I thank you from the bottom of my heart.

To my agent, Sheila Ableman, for believing in me and being there, whatever the circumstances. I appreciate this very much.

Finally, to my family, who have supported me throughout the writing of this book, a huge thank you. It has been an immensely traumatic, investigative journey, yet worth every single tear. I am extremely proud to have chronicled these harrowing stories, to demonstrate that such events are happening in front of us every day, all around us. Maybe now, we can open our eyes.

Further Help and Information

I have researched a few websites to offer support on the topics covered in the stories. If the addresses fail to upload on your computer, they can all be found using the 'Ask Jeeves' search engine. I hope you find them helpful:

Kareena

marriagepartner.com/talk/messages
Are young, teenage Asians forced into arranged, adult marriages, or happy to follow tradition? An interactive site, where you can enter into conversation, or simply read the views of other modern young Asians on arranged marriages.

Laura, Shannon

stopitnow.com
A site full of information and stories of hope for the survivors of child abuse.

alltheseyears.net

A site for the victims of rape, sexual and domestic abuse.

hiddenhurt.co.uk

A site for information on domestic abuse.

refuge.org.uk

A site for support and information on domestic violence

UK telephone number (a freephone helpline): 0808 200 0247

This is a helpline run in partnership between Women's Aid and Refuge. All advice given is confidential.

Grace

netdoctor.co.uk/womenshealth/features

This site defines empty nest syndrome, with examples and remedies.

Yasmine

redress.btinternet.co.uk/yaghill.htm

A shocking site about honour killings, full of information and true stories.

newswm.bbc.co.uk/l/hi/programmes/newsnight
The story of Surjit Athwal, a 26-year-old Indian from Hayes, Middlesex, who disappeared in India Punjab while on holiday in 1998.

Charlotte

anorexicweb.com
This is a very graphic, shocking site, with disturbing pictures of people suffering with anorexia nervosa. It is not recommended for children under the age of thirteen.

bodycage.com
A useful, informative site, created to inspire positive body image. Photos of anorexics are also included on the site.

Shy Girl

selfesteem4women.com
An excellent site to help build up confidence.

quotegarden.com/confidence
A site full of quotes to help you through your day and make you feel better about yourself.

mixedmarriage.net
An interactive site, with real articles, where visitors air their views and exchange experiences.

Tamara

babybumblebee.com
This site offers vocabulary-building DVDs in a set of ten, for speech and language development. Certainly worth a look, as they are very well recommended.

ddat.co.uk
This site provides information on a drug-free programme for children and adults with learning difficulties.

parentingyourcomplexchild.com
This is an interactive site, offering help, diagnosis, treatment and moral support for all problems you encounter during your journey through parenthood.

ninds.nih.gov/health_and_medical/pubs/autism.htm
This is an excellent informative site on all aspects of autism.